THE CASE AGAINST DIRECT ELECTION OF THE PRESIDENT

A Defense of the Electoral College

The Case Against
DIRECT ELECTION
OF THE PRESIDENT

A Defense of the Electoral College

by JUDITH BEST

Cornell University Press | ITHACA AND LONDON

First published 1975 by Cornell University Press.
Published in the United Kingdom by Cornell University Press Ltd.,
2-4 Brook Street, London W1Y 1AA.

International Standard Book Number 0-8014-0916-0
Library of Congress Catalog Card Number 74-25366 Feb. 26, 1975
Printed in the United States of America by York Composition Co., Inc.

To my children,
MICHAEL *and* DAVID

Contents

Tables

Acknowledgments

I am indebted to my teachers Walter Berns, Allan Sindler, and Allan Bloom for their encouragement, criticism, and guidance. Their devotion to academic freedom in trying times will remain an example to all their students.

J. B.

Ithaca, New York

THE CASE AGAINST
DIRECT ELECTION
OF THE PRESIDENT

A Defense of the
Electoral College

1 The Indictment Against the Electoral-College System

In August 1974, for the first time in the history of the republic, the office of President was occupied by a man who had not been confirmed by a national election. Gerald R. Ford, thirty-eighth President of the United States, succeeded to office on the resignation of his predecessor. Unlike vice-presidents who had succeeded before him, Gerald Ford was nominated by his predecessor and confirmed by the vote of Congress under the provisions for filling vice-presidential vacancies in the Twenty-fifth Amendment to the Constitution. Speaking to the American people in his inaugural address, President Ford stated, "I am acutely aware that you have not elected me as your President by your ballots."

In making this statement, the President clearly recognized the uniqueness of his incumbency and anticipated the attacks that might be made by majoritarian democrats on his mandate to govern. The consent of the governed is a necessary condition for the selection of leaders in a democracy. Democratic theory requires that consent be formally given in free and frequent elections. There is no question about Ford's legal and constitutional authority to govern. But many may question whether his theoretical legitimacy is compatible with the populistic principle that the man who fills the nation's highest office must be the choice of a majority of the people voting in secret ballot.

The Presidency is the republic's most visible and perhaps our most crucial institution. It is the only all-national office; only the President can claim to speak authoritatively for the nation. As the country's symbol of unity and continuity, as its "elective kingship," the Presidency has captured the imagination of the public and provided generations of political scientists and journalists with an unending drama to analyze, evaluate, and dissect.

In the decade between 1964 and 1974 the Presidency was subjected to very severe strains. In quick succession it was rocked by assassination, by the most unpopular war in the nation's history, by corruption and the abuse of power at the highest levels, by the first presidential resignation, and by the incumbency of the first man to attain the office without confirmation in a popular election. The institution was touched by death, disgrace, and disputed legitimacy. It is no wonder, then, that the events of the decade generated a national debate on limiting the powers of the Presidency, changing the nature of the office, and creating new devices to ensure that the office will be filled by men of ability and virtue.

One focus of this debate is the method of selecting presidents, since the manner of selection may have a profound influence on the kind of men who are chosen, on their conceptions of their proper roles, and on the popular acceptance of their legitimacy as leaders of a democratic republic. In 1969 and 1970, Congress considered a major reform of the presidential-election system: a proposal to amend the Constitution to abolish the electoral-college system and to replace it with a direct popular election of the President. Under the direct-election plan, the popular votes for President would be aggregated on a national level. Presently, popular votes are aggregated on a state level, and only electoral votes are aggregated nationally. The proponents of this election reform argued that both democratic theory and the needs of a modern technological society require a plebiscitary Presidency. The Ninety-first Congress ended without passing the election-reform amendment, but the issue is not dead. It remains on the national agenda as the debate on the Presidency accelerates.

The issue of how to choose a President is not new; rather, it has been the source of great and continuing controversy for nearly two hundred years. More constitutional amendments have been offered on the subject of presidential elections than on any other. Ironically, in the debates preceding the ratification of the Constitution, the mode of presidential selection was not controversial and, indeed, provided its authors some satisfaction. Alexander Hamilton, in *The Federalist*, wrote that "the mode of appointment of the chief magistrate of the United States is almost the only part of the system, of any consequence which has escaped without severe censure or which has received the slightest mark of approbation from its opponents." But severe censure was not long withheld.

The method of selection, as devised by the Founders, is an electoral college consisting of presidential electors who choose the President. The candidate who receives a majority of the electoral votes is elected; if no candidate receives a majority, the House of Representatives must, in a special contingency election, select the President from the top three candidates. According to the Constitution, each state may appoint, "in such Manner as the Legislature thereof may direct," as many electors as it has senators and representatives in Congress. In theory and in constitutional law, the states are free to choose presidential electors by whatever means they wish.

Initially, reform efforts were provoked by the diversity of methods employed by the state legislatures to select electors. It was felt that the varied and discordant methods of selection did not provide for fair expression of public opinion. Lack of uniformity increased the potential for abuse, as leading politicians of both parties were prompted "to rig the methods of choosing Presidential electors in their respective states to maximize their own electoral vote and minimize that of the opposition."[1] One option open to the state legislatures was to choose the electors themselves. This method was employed by a number of states in the early elections; South Carolina, in 1860, was the last state to abandon it.[2] With the rise of democratic sentiment, the practice was attacked as illegitimate, and the state legislatures began to adopt popular election as the most appropriate means of selecting electors. Once the popular-elec-

1. Neal Peirce, *The People's President: The Electoral College in American History and the Direct Vote Alternative* (New York, 1968), p. 65.

2. Peirce, *People's President*, pp. 309–311. All figures on the method of elector selection have been drawn from this source.

tion principle was widely accepted, the major issue became how to aggregate the votes of the people: by states (the unit-rule system, or general-ticket plan), by local districts (the district plan), or by party and by states (the proportional plan).

Most of the early reformers favored the district method of election. Necessity, however, proved more compelling than sentiment. In 1796, nine states chose electors either by a vote of their legislatures or by the unit-vote system, thus consolidating their electoral votes. Because the unit-vote method consolidates the electoral votes and the district plan disperses them, Madison introduced a bill in the Virginia legislature to shift from the district system to the unit-vote system.

As the unit rule, or general-ticket system, spread, reformers directed their fire against it, claiming, among other things, that it disfranchised minorities within a state and increased the influence of the large states. Despite several attempts in the first half of the nineteenth century to make the district system mandatory, it failed to muster sufficient support. Toward the end of the century, support for the proportional plan increased, because of a belief that it would most accurately reflect popular opinion in each state. In one of the early historical analyses of the electoral system, published in 1906, J. Hampden Dougherty, a leading advocate of the proportional plan, concluded that it was the only proposed reform not in conflict with the trend of institutional development in the United States.[3] By this

3. *The Electoral System of the United States* (New York, 1906).

time, largely because of the disputed election of 1876, the dangers inherent in the contingency election in the House were added to the list of charges against the electoral system.[4]

During the first half of this century, the reformers were, in the main, divided into two camps: those supporting the district plan, the mode favored by many of the Founders; and those favoring the proportional plan. Support for these plans peaked in the 1950's, when the reform groups managed to compromise their differences and produced a hybrid plan giving the states a choice between the two. This hybrid, the Mundt-Daniel plan, was cosponsored in 1956 by a bipartisan group of fifty-two senators. Only the skillful debate of Senators John Kennedy and Paul Douglas derailed the coalition movement in the Senate. Kennedy's strategy, in the words of James MacGregor Burns, was "to defeat a congressional party coalition with a presidential party coalition."[5] The core of Kennedy's argument, which has since been dubbed the counterweight argument, focused on the constitutional balance between the executive and the legislature. Kennedy conceded that the present system has an urban-liberal bias, but argued that it has served as a vital counterweight to the rural-conservative bias of the Congress. "It is not only the unit vote for the Presidency we are talking about, but a whole solar system of governmental power. If it is proposed to change the bal-

4. For a complete history of the reform proposals see Peirce, *People's President*, and Dougherty, *Electoral System*.
5. *The Deadlock of Democracy* (Englewood Cliffs, N.J., 1965), p. 305.

ance of power of one of the elements of the solar system, it is necessary to consider the others."[6] Kennedy and Douglas were highly persuasive, and no less than ten of the original sponsors withdrew their support.

Serious objections have been raised to both the district and the proportional plans.[7] Among other things, it has been persuasively argued that they would weaken the Presidency and the two-party system, localize presidential elections, and give strategic advantages to less populous, homogeneous states. Both lost support, though there remains a hard core of proponents of each. By the late 1960's a wave of sentiment favoring direct election developed. A number of polls recorded between 78 and 81 percent of the electorate in favor.

As a result, several election-reform bills were offered in both houses of Congress in 1969 and 1970. During the floor debate in the House, the results of a poll conducted by Senator Robert Griffin were offered as evidence of public support of a direct-election amendment. Senator Griffin polled four thousand state legislators; 64 percent of those responding favored direct election.[8] Senator Griffin's poll did not reveal whether support for direct election was so

6. *Congressional Record,* Vol. 102, Pt. 4, 84th Cong., 2d sess. (1956), p. 5150.

7. Allan P. Sindler, "Presidential Election Methods and Urban-Ethnic Interests," *Law and Contemporary Problems* 27 (1962), 213–233; Wallace S. Sayre and Judith H. Parris, *Voting for President: The Electoral College and the American Political System* (Washington, 1972), pp. 102–134.

8. *Congressional Record,* Vol. 115, Pt. 19, 91st Cong., 1st sess. (1969), p. 25126.

distributed among the state legislatures that ratification by the necessary three-fourths was assured, but the poll was significant because it indicated enough support to lessen congressional fears that the effort to pass a direct-election amendment might be an exercise in futility.

In September 1969, the House passed a direct-election amendment by the overwhelming vote of 339 to 70—a favorable vote of 78 percent of the total membership. This was the first time the House had considered a direct election amendment at length, and the first time since 1854 that it seriously considered altering the presidential electoral system. One year later the Senate considered a practically identical constitutional amendment. The question was never brought to a vote in the Senate, as two attempts to close debate failed. The movement to add a direct-election amendment to the Constitution had been stopped for the moment, but many advocates of the amendment hope to put it back on the congressional agenda in the near future.

A number of factors have changed the direction of election reform. In 1960 and 1968, the elections were so close that fears of electoral misfire were aroused. Indeed, in 1960 it was questioned whether Kennedy actually had the popular plurality, owing to the great difficulties in determining his popular vote in Alabama.[9] In 1968, the Wallace candidacy, one of the strongest third-party movements since 1860, rekindled fears of electoral-college deadlock and of the possible need to use the contingency procedure for the first time in nearly 150 years. Furthermore, in recent elec-

9. Peirce, *People's President*, p. 102.

tions there has been a recurring tendency for electors to assert their constitutional independence. In 1960, Henry D. Irwin, a Republican elector pledged to Nixon in Oklahoma, not only violated his trust but also took part in a national movement to subvert the results of the popular election in favor of some conservative candidate.[10] Finally, the Supreme Court's reapportionment decisions of the early 1960's, with their ringing principle of one man, one vote, were believed to have effectively rebutted the counterweight argument. A moderate reform, the automatic plan, which would retain the electoral count but not the electors, had been supported by the Johnson administration and originally sponsored by Senator Birch Bayh. It was no longer seriously considered after the prestigious American Bar Association adopted its special commission's report on direct election. Senator Bayh and Congressman Emanuel Celler sponsored the ABA's direct-election proposal in the form of joint resolutions. Celler successfully steered his bill through the House, an action he considers one of the most significant in his long career.

The proponents of direct election claim that it is an idea whose time has come. Their case is apparently a strong one, and it incorporates almost two centuries of criticism against the present system. The indictment, as stated in the report of the ABA commission, is that the "electoral college method of electing a President of the United States is

10. U.S., Senate, Committee on the Judiciary, Subcommittee on Constitutional Amendments, *Hearings, Nomination and Election of President and Vice President and Qualifications for Voting*, 87th Cong., 1st sess., 1961, p. 446.

archaic, undemocratic, complex, ambiguous, indirect and dangerous."[11] The electoral-college system, it is claimed, does not guarantee that the candidate with the most popular votes will win, produces great inequalities in voting power among the national electorate, contains a contingency-election provision that is not only unrepresentative but that could also result in an impasse or in political deals, permits the will of the majority voters in a state or even in the nation to be thwarted through the constitutional independence of the electors, and permits the electoral decision to turn on fraud or chance in key states. These charges are more complex than this brief indictment indicates and must be examined in greater detail.

The present system is an amalgam of constitutional and conventional rules. A commonplace of political analysis is that the electoral college has never worked as the Founders intended. The system has evolved in the course of our history, and changes have occurred mainly through customary, not constitutional, revision. At least three charges in the indictment against the present system can be directly attributed to a conventional rule.

The method of aggregating votes in force today, variously called the general-ticket, the unit-rule, or the winner-take-all system, is a conventional rule that was used by a few states in the first elections and spread rapidly to all the other states. Under the provisions of the unit rule, the

11. U.S., Senate, Committee on the Judiciary, Subcommittee on Constitutional Amendments, *Hearings, Election of the President*, 89th Cong., 2d sess., and 90th Cong., 1st sess., 1968, p. 21 (cited hereafter as 1968 Senate *Hearings*).

candidate winning a statewide popular plurality gets all of that state's electoral votes. The unit rule spread because it was favorable to the majority party in each state, and because those states that did not consolidate their electoral power were believed to have less influence and less strength in an election than those that did consolidate.

There is only one minor exception to the universality of the unit rule. In 1969, Maine, which presently has four electoral votes, changed its system. Two of its electoral votes go to the candidate with a plurality in the state as a whole. One of the remaining two votes goes to the candidate carrying one of its two congressional districts, and one to the candidate carrying the other. Thus, one of Maine's electoral votes may be different from the other three.

Although theoretically the unit system could be abandoned by the states at any time, in practice it is not likely to be changed unless there is a constitutional amendment, for the same reasons that led to its universal adoption. Several states, mostly small ones, would prefer a district system because it would divide the huge blocs of electoral votes possessed by the large states. They believe, however, that they cannot afford to switch on their own. In an effort to change the system, Delaware and other states brought suit, as *parens patriae,* against New York. This suit challenged the constitutionality of the state unit system as a denial of due process and equal protection and asked the Supreme Court for declaratory and injunctive relief, suggesting that no other remedy was available to citizens whose votes in presidential elections are "diluted, debased and misappropriated."[12] Delaware wanted the Court to declare the unit rule unconstitutional and thereby open the door to the district system, although there were some states that indicated they would find the proportional system acceptable. The Supreme Court refused to hear this case.

But even if the Court had entertained the suit and ruled against the unit system, it could not have abolished the electoral college, since the Constitution assigns electoral votes to the states. Thus, it could not have resolved all the objections to the present system. The district and proportional plans, though still backed by some members of Congress, are no longer under serious consideration. Therefore the indictment against the present system must be considered in terms of the only reform that currently has a chance of being adopted, the direct-election plan.

The first charge in the indictment, believed by many to be an unanswerable objection, is that the present system not only may allow, but actually has allowed, the election of a runner-up President. In three elections the candidate who polled a popular plurality was declared the loser. However, because of unusual circumstances affecting two of these elections, there is disagreement among the reformers on the number of runner-up presidents actually produced by the electoral college. For example, Congressman Celler counts the victors in the elections of 1824, 1876, and 1888: John Quincy Adams, Rutherford Hayes, and

12. *Delaware* v. *New York*, 385 U.S. 895 (1966); brief for plaintiff reprinted in 1968 Senate *Hearings*, p. 808.

Benjamin Harrison.[13] On the other hand, Senator Bayh counts only Harrison.[14] The evidence supports Senator Bayh's position. In 1824, John Quincy Adams was elected by the House, although Andrew Jackson had a popular plurality of approximately 37,000 votes. There were four candidates, and no one received a majority of the electoral votes. But in six states with 71 electoral votes, or 27 percent of the total, the state legislatures chose the electors. There is no way to determine the total popular vote in 1824, and therefore no way to conclude that Jackson was deprived of a popular victory. Furthermore, this election is not representative of the functionings of the present system, since not only did six states employ the legislative method of selection, but six other states used the district system. Half of the twenty-four states were not operating under the present system. Although the statistical histories give Tilden the plurality over Hayes in the election of 1876, it is difficult to assert with any confidence that he actually surpassed Hayes in the popular vote, since both sides engaged in widespread fraud in casting and counting the votes. Whether the electoral system actually produced three runner-up presidents or one, the fact remains that it did clearly and unequivocally produce one. Harrison defeated Cleveland in the electoral college but not in the popular vote.

The possibility of a runner-up President has been built

13. *Congressional Record,* Vol. 115, Pt. 18, 91st Cong., 1st sess. (1969), p. 24963.

14. 1968 Senate *Hearings,* p. 21.

into the system through both constitutional and customary rules. It derives from the constitutional formula of awarding each state three electoral votes regardless of its population, from the fact that voter turnout does not change the allotment of electoral votes, and from the unit rule, which eliminates intrastate minority votes at the preliminary level. In 1969, the chairman of the House Committee on the Judiciary, Emanuel Celler, described the prospect of a runner-up Presidency as "horrible, unsporting, dangerous and downright uncivilized."[15] Fears were voiced by many congressmen that the country would not tolerate another President who had received fewer popular votes than his opponent.

But the case against the present system does not rely on the runner-up Presidency of Benjamin Harrison alone. There have been a number of very close elections in our history; Congressman Celler and Neal Peirce, among many others, have argued that the nation has come too close to electing the popular-vote loser in several elections in which the popular-vote margin between the major candidates was 3 percent or less. It is contended that in some of these elections a shift of less than 1 percent of the popular votes in strategic states would have produced a runner-up President. Neal Peirce lists twenty elections between 1824 and 1964 in which minor vote shifts could have changed the outcome.[16]

The principle underlying the charge that the present

---

15. *Congressional Record*, Vol. 115, Pt. 18, 91st Cong., 1st sess. (1969), p. 24963.

16. *People's President*, p. 317.

system may result in the victory of a runner-up is that democratic legitimacy requires a guarantee that the candidate with the most popular votes will win. The proponents of a direct popular election argue that only such an election can provide that guarantee.

Another charge is that the present system produces great inequalities in popular voting power. The plaintiffs in *Delaware* v. *New York* claimed that the minority voters in each state are denied their political right to associate meaningfully across state lines in national elections, and that the minority votes are misappropriated and given to the majority voters in each state.[17] Simply stated, this aspect of the charge is that under the present system intrastate minorities are disfranchised. The unit rule, or in the critics' terminology, the winner-take-all rule, is responsible for this inequity. Classic form was given to this objection by Senator Thomas Hart Benton in 1824: "To lose their votes is the fate of all minorities, and it is their duty to submit; but this is not a case of votes lost, but of votes taken away, added to those of the majority, and given to a person to whom the minority is opposed."[18]

In addition to disfranchising the intrastate minority, the critics assert, the unit rule in some cases has created situations in which a majority have not really had their votes counted—at least in one sense. This may happen in a three-way race in which candidate *A* receives 40 percent of the popular vote; candidate *B*, 35 percent; and candidate *C*, 25 percent. Candidate *A* receives 100 percent of the electoral

17. 1968 Senate *Hearings*, p. 808.
18. Quoted by Neal Peirce in *People's President*, p. 152.

votes; therefore, 60 percent of the people in the state are disfranchised. Proponents claim that the direct election, by eliminating the electoral votes, will correct these defects.

Closely related to the complaint about intrastate voting inequities is the claim that a direct popular election will strengthen the two-party system. The proponents note that under the present system minority voters are not only disfranchised, but in one-party states they are almost permanently locked in. It is argued that there is little incentive in such states for the minority party to campaign vigorously, since, in terms of electoral votes, there are no rewards forthcoming either immediately or in the near future. Thus, it is suggested, the present system tends to perpetuate one-party dominance in some states. The advocates of direct election foresee a potential for the growth of minority parties under the reform, because their efforts would be materially rewarded. Every vote within a state would be a prize worth the expenditure of campaign resources, because all the votes, including those for the statewide minority party, would count directly at the national level, and no vote would be "lost" at the preliminary statewide level. Furthermore, proponents claim that when the result of a statewide election is a foregone conclusion, even the members of the majority party have less incentive to vote. Advocates anticipate that a direct election will encourage the democratic ideal of participation and will stimulate voter interest.

Another aspect of the voter-inequality charge concerns interstate voting inequities. Under the Constitution each state is allotted as many electors as it has representatives in the Congress; thus each state is guaranteed at least three electoral votes. These votes are the so-called bonus votes and are deviations from the straight population principle. Hence Alaska, with a population of 300,000, has three electoral votes, or one for every 100,000 people, whereas New York, with a population of 18,000,000, has only forty-one electoral votes, or one for every 440,000 people. All other things being equal, there would appear to be an advantage for voters in small states.

Some critics argue that it is not the voters in small states but the voters in large competitive states who have the advantage in voting power. They point out that candidates and campaign managers operate under the following rule of thumb: campaign in large doubtful states. In support of their argument, these critics of the electoral system cite the results of a computer analysis by John F. Banzhaf III,[19] who concludes:

Far from favoring the smaller States the existing electoral college system actually discriminates against voters in the small and middle-sized States by giving the citizens of the few large States an excessive amount of voting power. Citizens of States like New York and California actually have over 2½ times as much chance to affect the election of the President as residents of some of the smaller States and more than three times as much chance as citizens of the District of Columbia.[20]

19. John F. Banzhaf III, "One Man, 3.312 Votes: A Mathematical Analysis of the Electoral College," *Villanova Law Review* 13 (1968), 304.

20. Statement of John F. Banzhaf III; in U.S., House of Representatives, Committee on the Judiciary, *Hearings, Electoral College Reform*, 91st Cong., 1st sess., 1969, p. 353 (cited hereafter as 1969 House *Hearings*).

The reason for this discrimination is that under the unit rule a presidential ballot is cast for a bloc of electoral votes. Each voter in New York potentially influences forty-one electoral votes, and each voter in the District of Columbia potentially influences three electoral votes. Opponents of the unit rule claim it does much more than cancel the advantage of voters in small states; they believe it creates an advantage for voters in large states. They find this voting-power advantage reflected in the way presidential campaigns are conducted, since most of the campaign resources in money and time are spent in the large states; they also find it reflected in the principle of candidate selection. Presidential candidates have been overwhelmingly the citizens of large states. Of the seventy major party candidates in the thirty-five election contests between 1836 (when the system of nominating candidates by general party conventions began) and 1972, thirty-two have come from New York or Ohio, while twenty-eight states have never had one of their favorite sons in serious contention for the Presidency.

But it is not the mere fact of this interstate advantage to citizens in large states that most disturbs some of the reformers. Rather, it is the belief that this advantage often results in an intrastate advantage to tightly organized, highly disciplined, special-interest groups who may hold the balance of power in a state. The advantage to these special-interest groups is compounded when the state in which they hold the balance of power is a key state in the election. This particular inequity was cited by many congressmen as one of the most grievous defects in the present system. In the House debates, Congressman Clark Mac-Gregor of Minnesota quoted Mr. Wekselman, spokesman for the American Jewish Congress, who frankly admitted that the Jewish "vote is maximized under the present system because our people concentrate in the bigger cities of America."[21] Congressman MacGregor opposed "weighting the vote in favor of anybody"; he did not want to see "this House subscribe to any other system which would perpetuate the unequal strength given to some of these tightly organized special-interest groups."[22] Although this advantage can be exaggerated, there is some basis for it. In several elections New York, which has been, from our earliest days, one of the advantaged states (according to Banzhaf's calculations), was so evenly divided between the two major parties that a small group held the balance of power in the state. Among these elections were those of 1844, when the Liberty party held the balance, and 1884, when the independents, or Mugwumps, held the balance.

Another voting-power inequity arises from the fact that electoral votes in excess of the three guaranteed each state are awarded to the states according to their populations as determined in the decennial census. But the population of a state varies from election year to election year, and in at least two elections and possibly in three, the actual population may differ markedly from the official population as recorded in electoral votes. Those states with diminishing populations have a temporary advantage. Moreover, since

21. *Congressional Record*, Vol. 115, Pt. 19, 91st Cong., 1st sess. (1969), p. 25149.
22. *Ibid.*

the actual population differs from the voting population, it is charged that there often is a bonus for nonvoters. That is, if a state has a low turnout, the voters in that state have more voting power than those in a state of similar size but with a high turnout.

There are, then, three main deviations from the principle of equality in the present system. One favors the small states, one the low-turnout states, and one the large pivotal states. But the advantages do not totally offset each other. The proponents of direct election argue that each and every vote cast in an election should have the same weight, and that each citizen has an individual interest in combining his vote with the votes of those who share his sentiments, wherever they may reside within the electorate as a whole. In the House debates, Congressman MacGregor stated that the fundamental point was "the right to cast an absolutely equally weighted vote."[23] Advocates of direct election argue that the rules should not be rigged in any-one's favor and that only a direct election can implement this right to an equally weighted vote.

The third major charge in the indictment against the present system is addressed to the provisions for a contingency election. The Constitution requires that, to be elected, a candidate must have a majority of the electoral votes. Any election system which does not give the victory to the winner of the simple plurality must contain a contingency-election procedure in order to achieve its objective of filling the office. The complaint against the present system, in which the House chooses among the three top

23. *Ibid.*

contenders, with each state casting one vote, no matter how many congressmen it has, is that it is undemocratic, unjust, and impractical.

It is undemocratic because the election process is removed from the people, and because the winner of the popular plurality might not be selected by the House. Lucius Wilmerding argues: "If the popular principle is the true principle of this election, as indicated by the Constitution itself, nothing can be more absurd than to abandon it entirely as soon as the People, at first effort, fail to give a majority of votes for one candidate. It is like punishing the People, by forfeiture, for not being more unanimous."[24]

The contingency system is said to be unjust because a state delegation may be equally divided and therefore that state could not cast its vote. Another injustice is that a state with one representative has a vote equal to that of a state with forty-three representatives. The five smallest states, with a combined population of two million, would have the same voting power as the five largest states, with a combined population of seventy-two million.

The system is impractical because it could produce a President and a Vice-President of different political parties, since the Vice-President is not chosen by the House but by the Senate. It is also impractical because of the possibility that no candidate will receive a majority within the requisite number of days. If a deadlock continued for seventeen days after the Congress convened, the nation would be left with the newly selected Vice-President as acting President or, if a Vice-President could not be chosen, the Speaker of

24. *The Electoral College* (New Brunswick, N.J., 1958), p. 185.

the House as acting President. There is also the possibility that the incumbent President would be urged to continue in office until the deadlock could be resolved. The situation could degenerate into a Pope, anti-Pope affair. And, if all this were not enough, it is charged that a contingency election would be unsavory, because it might lead to political intrigue; bargains and compromises might be made between the candidates or their men in the House in return for support. In 1824, the last time the House was called upon to decide, Henry Clay, who was eliminated from House consideration because he was the candidate with the fourth highest electoral count, gave his support to John Q. Adams, who was thereafter selected. When President Adams named Clay his Secretary of State, the Jacksonians decried the "corrupt bargain." True or not, the Adams administration was shadowed by these charges of a political deal, and Adams himself was the subject of vicious attacks. The mere appearance, if not the reality, of a backroom deal may damage the Presidency.

To the debaters in the House, the potential for political intrigue was not merely the ghost of a century past but a barely averted reality of the preceding election. In the public-opinion polls in autumn 1968, the rising percentage for George Wallace (from 16 percent in June to 21 percent in mid-September) frightened many political and congressional leaders. As the percentage for Wallace rose, so did the possibility of a House election and the specter of vote-trading for commitments on future policy.

The direct-popular-election plan contains a contingency provision that many proponents believe will cure the disorders of the present system. The provision would eliminate the undemocratic elements by abandoning the federal principle in the contingency election. They claim their proposal, which provides for a run-off if no candidate obtains a 40 percent plurality, would restore popular control over the selection process, ensure the victory of the candidate with a plurality, reduce the potential for political deals, and practically eliminate the possibility of an impasse.

The fourth major charge in the indictment relates to the constitutional office of presidential elector. The electors are the only citizens who vote directly for the President. The role intended for the electors by the Founders has been debated for over a century. One interpretation often suggested by the reformers is that the Founders, fearing the mob, intended the electors to be totally independent because the people as a whole were unfit to make a rational choice. It is rather easy to score points against the present system by arguing that the country has outgrown the need for a council of wise men established by those who feared the unruly and unfit masses, but it is unfair: first, because the system has never operated in that fashion, and second because such sentiments cannot be attributed to the Founders as a whole nor to their intention in establishing the electoral college. One group of scholars claims the college was first and foremost a compromise that attempted to give something to everybody. To placate those who feared congressional selection, it gave the power to appoint electors to the state legislatures; to the large states it gave a modified principle of popular representation; to the small states it gave the bonus votes and the provision for selection by states in the House contingency plan; to those who favored the popular election of electors it opened that possibility through the action of their own state legislatures.

Lucius Wilmerding, who believes the electors were not intended to be mere agents or rubber stamps (they were, after all, to vote by ballot, presumably secretly), concludes that "it is very doubtful that these electors were intended to act a part wholly independent of the people."[25] Others have made the same contention,[26] but the case has been most convincingly argued by Wilmerding, who relies on the discussions in the Federal Convention and on the fact that originally the electors were required to name not one, but two, men, and they were not authorized to distinguish between their choices for President and Vice-President. The expectation was that one of the two men named would be the state's favorite son, and the other a continental char-acter—the people's presumptive favorite. In addition, the records of the convention indicate that "the electoral sys-tem was the invention, not of that part of the federal con-vention which distrusted the people, but of that part which trusted them."[27]

A different interpretation is given by Paul Eidelberg, who argues that congressional selection was opposed be-cause the Founders feared the possibility of intrigue and corruption between congressmen and candidates for the

25. *Ibid.*, p. 171.
26. See John P. Roche, "The Electoral College: A Note on American Political Mythology," *Dissent* 8 (1961), 197; and Clin-ton Rossiter, *The American Presidency* (New York, 1964).
27. Wilmerding, *Electoral College*, p. 171.

Presidency. The same objection was raised against selection by the state governors and by electors chosen by the states when it was assumed they would all meet at the nation's capital. Eidelberg contends that the members of the convention wished to insulate the election from the process of political negotiation. It was to be insulated, not only from the people, but also from the influence of their leaders in the states as well as from their leaders in the Congress, who were expressly excluded from the office of elector. Finally, it was to be insulated against intrigue among the electors themselves, since they were not to meet in one place as a deliberative body.[28]

Whether the electoral college was a compromise designed to give something to everyone, or whether it embodied a principle and was designed to "secure the independence and integrity of the President by making it extremely difficult for Presidential candidates to court their electors,"[29] the electoral college was not a slur on the character of the people as opposed to their leaders.

Regardless of which of the interpretations of the Founders' intentions is the true one, the college has not operated as originally intended, and the original conception now serves only as the focal point for debaters' rhetoric. As our system evolved, other agencies, the political parties, through their national party conventions, have taken over and transformed the function of the electoral college.

28. Paul Eidelberg, "The Presidency and Its Intended Role in American Political Life," in *The Philosophy of the American Constitution* (New York, 1968).

29. *Ibid.*, p. 172.

The substantive charge against the present system is that the office of elector is potentially dangerous because in a close election a few renegade electors could frustrate the will of the majority. Although no election has been stolen by faithless electors, a few electors have disregarded the expressed will of the voters in their states, effectively misappropriating their votes. The electors normally cast their votes for the winners in their states, and are considered morally bound to do so. In most states, however, they are not legally bound, and even when they are, there seems to be no way to compel the electors to honor their pledges. In *Ray* v. *Blair*, the Supreme Court held that an elector may be required to pledge himself to vote for a given candidate, but the enforceability of this pledge is constitutionally dubious.[30]

It could be argued that since the Constitution gives unlimited discretion to the state legislatures in appointing the electors, it is also within their power to bind the electors. A counterargument can be deduced from the original intention and from the fact that the electors were expected to vote by secret ballot.[31] After the Oklahoma Republican elector Henry Irwin cast his vote for Harry Flood Byrd in 1960, the state legislature provided for a fine of one thousand dollars for any elector who failed to support his party's candidates. Even if the electors may be charged under penalty to honor their pledges, it would seem that the

30. *Ray* v. *Blair*, 343 U.S. 214 (1952).
31. Robert G. Dixon, Jr., "Electoral College Procedure," *Western Political Quarterly* 3 (June 1950), 214.

state's only recourse is to impose the penalty. There is grave doubt that the state could change the vote.

In 1969, Congressman James G. O'Hara of Michigan and Senator Edmund Muskie of Maine challenged the vote of a North Carolina elector during the joint congressional session that formally counted the electoral votes. The challenge, the first in ninety-two years, was based on the statute enacted by the Congress in 1887 in response to the Hayes-Tilden dispute, which is currently part of the United States Code.[32] Under the statute both houses, acting concurrently, may reject an electoral vote if they agree that it has not been "regularly given" and "lawfully certified." The challenge was unsuccessful, and the vote of Dr. Lloyd Bailey, a Republican elector who disregarded the mandate of the voters in his state (though not in his district) by voting for George Wallace, was counted as cast.

The first case of a faithless elector occurred in 1796, when Samuel Miles, a Federalist elector, voted for Jefferson, thereby provoking the now famous retort: "Do I chuse Samuel Miles to determine for me whether John Adams or Thomas Jefferson shall be President? No! I chuse him to act, not to think."[33] The most recent instance occurred in 1972, when Roger McBride of Charlottesville, Virginia, a Republican elector, cast his vote for Libertarian party candidate John Hospers, as a protest against increasing federal control over the direction of American lives. Accounts of

32. U.S. Code, Title 3, Section 15.
33. Quoted in Edward Stanwood, *A History of Presidential Elections* (Boston, 1884), p. 51.

the number of faithless electors differ because of the difficulty of determining whether some electors of the past century were actually pledged to vote for but one candidate. Accounts range from four to eight, with seven the most generally accepted figure. Although the number of faithless electors is not large, the moral outrage they arouse must be considered, because it has a direct bearing on the popular appraisal of the electoral system.

The recent rise in the incidence of faithless electors (four in the last five elections) has been accompanied by the less odious but also problematic unpledged-elector movement. Unpledged electors cannot be considered betrayers or traitors, but they are often potential spoilers. The first modern use of unpledged electors followed from the Dixiecrat strategy of 1948. The Dixiecrats hoped to prevent an initial majority in the electoral college, obtain the balance of power, and then wring policy concessions from one of the major candidates in return for support either in the electoral college or in the House. In 1960, the unpledged-elector movement adopted the same strategy and won fourteen electoral votes in two southern states, Alabama and Mississippi. The closeness of the election tempted the unpledged electors to appeal to pledged electors to withhold their votes from John F. Kennedy and throw the election into the House, where it was hoped that a possible coalition of Southern Democrats and Republicans might elect a more conservative candidate.

It is argued that the system of presidential electors is a potential danger to the two-party system because it encourages this type of third-party strategy. The constitutional independence of electors can place the balance of power, and therefore the power to dictate the choice of President, in the hands of a regionally based minority party, and it can produce political deals after the general election. There must always be coalition-building, but our tradition has been to create coalitions prior to the general election in order that the people may ratify them. The direct-election plan would abolish the office of elector and thereby eliminate the problem of the faithless elector and the third-party strategy which relies on the existence of the college.

The last charge in the indictment against the electoral system is that the unit rule places a premium on fraud and chance because an entire election can hinge on a few popular votes in a pivotal state. The proponents of direct election do not claim that their reform will prevent all fraudulent practices but, rather, that it will reduce the temptation to engage in fraud because it will reduce the potential rewards. Congressman Abner Mikva argues that "the less leverage there is, the less fraud there can be, and the direct election plan has the least leverage of all."[34]

In 1960 there were allegations of irregularities in the state of Illinois, where only 9,000 votes separated the two major candidates and 27 electoral votes were in the balance. The electoral votes of this state, together with those of four other states in which the election was closely contested would have changed the final result.

It is argued, further, that random events such as rainstorms, power failures, and epidemics may swing an entire

34. *Congressional Record*, Vol. 115, Pt. 19, 91st Cong., 1st sess. (1969), p. 25134.

election if they occur in strategic states. In the election of 1884, one of the closest in our history, there was a driving rainstorm in upstate New York, a Republican stronghold, and thus good weather for Democrats. Cleveland, the Democratic candidate, won the key state of New York by a plurality of 1,149 votes, and with New York he won the election. The reformers argue that a direct election would remove the premium for fraud and chance because it would eliminate the unit vote.

The case for direct election rests on the following assertions: it is the only truly democratic method of election, it is the only proposed reform that remedies all the cited defects of the present system, and it is the only reform that has any chance of congressional passage. The 1968 election and in particular the strength of the Wallace candidacy have shaken politicians throughout the country. The frequent reports of Wallace's activities since then and speculations about his intentions for 1976 continue to be matters of concern. The reformers have coalesced; they may disagree about particular modes of reform, but their agreement that there must be some type of reform has overshadowed and, in most cases, overcome their differences. George Meany, in his testimony before the House Committee on the Judiciary, expressed his judgment that "almost anything would be preferable to the present system."[35] The statements by the overwhelming majority of debaters in the House indicated the urgency felt by the members. Even those who offered or supported substitute plans stated openly that if their plans were not accepted they would,

35. 1969 House *Hearings,* p. 520.

and eventually they in fact did, support the committee's direct-election plan.

When the American Bar Association house of delegates met, prior to their vote endorsing the direct-election plan, they were told by Edward W. Kuhn, the immediate past president, that they should vote for the direct plan because it was the only reform which had any chance in Congress.[36] Whether this was a self-fulfilling prophecy or an accurate assessment of the situation is difficult to prove. In any event, the district plan fell in the House to a teller vote of 159 to 192. The automatic plan, which would have retained the electoral votes but not the office of elector, fell to a teller vote of 64 to 98, and the proportional plan to a teller vote of 147 to 179.

Serious objections have been raised to both the district and the proportional plans.[37] The district plan tows in its wake the seemingly insurmountable problem of gerrymandering. The proportional plan (and the district plan as well) could produce fundamental changes in political alignments. Allan Sindler suggests that the proportional plan could increase the South's political influence and, furthermore, result in a tendency toward predominant one-partyism.[38] Many critics of the present system object to the automatic plan, since it would freeze the unit rule, which they consider the worst defect of the system, into the Con-

36. *Congressional Record*, Vol. 115, Pt. 19, 91st Cong., 1st sess. (1969), p. 25626.

37. Sindler, "Election Methods," p. 224; Sayre and Parris, *Voting for President*, pp. 102–134.

38. Sindler, "Election Methods," p. 224.

stitution. Since each of the alternative plans retains the electoral vote, the proponents of direct election argue that the plans would produce only partial reforms. Under each of them a runner-up President is possible, and the voting-power inequities are not totally eliminated.

The case for a direct election appears to be strong, and the list of anticipated benefits is imposing: (1) It would guarantee that the winner of the popular vote would win the office. (2) It would give each citizen an equally weighted vote regardless of where he lived and how his neighbors voted. (3) It would place the contingency election in the hands of the people. (4) It would eliminate faithless and unpledged electors. (5) It would reduce the premium on fraud and chance. (6) It would strengthen the two-party system. (7) It would stimulate voter interest and participation. A question before the nation is whether the direct-election system is preferable to the present one. This is not to suggest that no other reform is desirable or possible, but rather that the direct-election plan has captured the field of election reform. And until its status as a panacea can be effectively rebutted, it will continue to monopolize the reform movement.

A direct presidential election would constitute a fundamental change in our established institutions. As many of the proponents would agree, the fact that the present system has worked for some time creates a presumption in favor of continuing it. They believe they have proved the fallacy of that presumption and have established the desirability of their proposed reform above all others. Their arguments against the present system are often powerful;

their case for a direct election is seemingly persuasive; but the arguments must be scrutinized and the case examined. The issue is at once simple and fundamental: it is the issue of leadership selection in this large, diverse federal republic. Who will the leaders be? What kind of men will be selected? What factors will influence their conduct? To whose needs will they be sensitive? The answers to these questions are directly related to the mode of selection. The change proposed is fundamental and could have far-reaching effects on the entire political system. It could affect the two-party system, the national-convention system, federalism, the relationship between our executive and legislative institutions, and the very character of the Presidency. Such changes should not be lightly or blithely made. If something is really wrong with our system, we must change it; if it requires a cure, we must find a remedy. But since every change has unforeseeable side effects, we must proceed with caution. It is, then, fitting that in considering whether the case for direct election is compelling, we remember the words of Washington in his Farewell Address:

In all changes to which you may be invited, remember that time and habit are at least as necessary to fix the true character of government as of other human institutions; that experience is the surest standard by which to test the real tendency of the existing constitution of a country; that facility in changes, upon the credit of mere hypothesis and opinion exposes to perpetual change, from the endless variety of hypothesis and opinion.

2 The Runner-up Presidency

The unanswerable objection to the present system, according to many of its critics, is the fact that it may give us a President who is not the choice of a majority or a plurality of the voters. This apparently unanswerable objection arises from the populistic principle of the unlimited sovereignty of the majority, which Robert A. Dahl has described as the "only rule compatible with decision-making in a populistic democracy."[1] Although there are various reasons why strict adherence to this rule is undesirable, many critics seem to believe that the objection to a minority President need only be stated, not argued. As Dahl comments, however, "it may be impossible to find a voting method that satisfies the Rule and at the same time meets certain practical requirements."[2] The majority principle can be a very stringent requirement in a heterogeneous republic which also supports reasonably free access to inclusion on the ballot. We are unwilling to limit strictly the number of candidates on the ballot; we want a single election; yet having more than two candidates on the ballot

1. *A Preface to Democratic Theory* (Chicago, 1956), p. 37.
2. *Ibid.*, p. 43.

sharply reduces the likelihood that any one of them will poll a majority.

In its pure or unmodified form the populistic principle denies the legitimacy of all minority presidents, not to mention the legitimacy of Gerald Ford, the only President who has not been confirmed by a national election. Whatever the merits or demerits of this rule, the fact remains (as Table 1 indicates) that the republic has experienced fifteen

Table 1. Percentage of popular vote received by minority presidents and their closest opponents

Year	President	Percentage	Closest opponent	Percentage
1824	Adams	30.54	Jackson	43.13
1844	Polk	49.56	Clay	48.14
1848	Taylor	47.35	Cass	42.52
1856	Buchanan	45.32	Frémont	33.13
1860	Lincoln	39.78	Douglas	29.49
1876	Hayes	48.04	Tilden	50.99
1880	Garfield	48.32	Hancock	48.21
1884	Cleveland	48.53	Blaine	48.24
1888	Harrison	47.86	Cleveland	48.66
1892	Cleveland	46.04	Harrison	43.01
1912	Wilson	41.85	T. Roosevelt	27.42
1916	Wilson	49.26	Hughes	46.12
1948	Truman	49.51	Dewey	45.13
1960	Kennedy	49.48	Nixon	49.32
1968	Nixon	43.40	Humphrey	42.70

Source: Figures for all tables were computed from the election statistics in Svend Petersen, *A Statistical History of the American Presidential Elections* (New York, 1968).

terms of minority presidencies since its founding. Theoretically, these fifteen terms lacked some measure of democratic legitimacy. The word "legitimacy" is derived from the Latin *legitimis*, meaning lawful, but in ordinary usage today the term means sanctioned by law or custom, reasonable, logically correct. Unquestionably, these presidential terms were legitimate in the sense of being lawful, but it is questionable that, according to the populistic rule, they were logically correct.

Whatever our final judgment on the populistic theory, the nation's experience with minority presidencies illustrates the tension between theory and practice, for at least seven of these fifteen presidential terms have been ranked among the most notable in our history: the terms of Polk, Lincoln, Cleveland (two), Wilson (two), and Truman.[3] These five men have attained a place among the ten greatest presidents. Indeed, the man who reached the office after receiving the lowest popular percentage in our history (Lincoln with 39.78 percent) is widely acclaimed as the greatest of all our presidents, and his only rival for the position is George Washington.[4] On the other hand, the two presidencies often ranked at the bottom, those of Grant and Harding (the latter has been called a "near disaster for the Presidency"),[5] were won with high popular percentages. Grant won his second term with 55.6 percent of the

3. Clinton Rossiter, *The American Presidency* (New York, 1964), p. 100.

4. John Q. Adams did indeed receive a lower percentage of the popular vote, but in six states the legislatures chose the electors. It should also be noted that Lincoln's name did not appear on the ballot in ten states.

5. Rossiter, *American Presidency*, p. 101.

popular vote, and Harding won his single term with 60.3 percent, the fourth highest in our history.[6]

In more modern times, Lyndon Johnson, who had won office in 1964 by an extraordinary majority of the popular vote, although he was a sitting President was driven, in 1968, to renounce what would ordinarily have been a certain second nomination because of a climate of growing distrust and vilification. The man who won the highest popular vote percentage of all, Richard Nixon, in 1972, is the only President who resigned from office, and he did so under threat of impeachment and conviction. These stark facts have led many political analysts to conclude that a landslide victory may be undesirable and dysfunctional because it removes a political check on the Presidency. The plebiscitary Presidency may foster or release the power of arrogance. At the very least, the contrast between our successful minority presidencies and our unsuccessful "plebiscitary" ones illustrates Tocqueville's point about the tensions between the unlimited sovereignty of the majority and the pursuit of excellence and the common good. Finally, the widespread acceptance of the legitimacy of the Ford Presidency, which came into being without a popular election to obtain the formal consent of the governed, demonstrates that when theory is confronted by the necessities of practice, it is the former which must bend.

6. All figures on electoral and popular vote percentages have been taken or computed from the raw data on presidential elections in Svend Petersen, *A Statistical History of the American Presidential Elections* (New York, 1968).

To be sure, the unanswerable objection to the present system is not merely that it produces minority presidents, but rather that it can produce a particular type of minority President, the runner-up President. However, concern among the reformers about the wisdom of permitting any kind of minority Presidency is sufficient (as indicated in the House debates) to warrant some discussion of the problem. Furthermore, although the objection to runner-up presidents is deduced from the principle of majority rule, the power and prestige of the Presidency derive as much from the nature and character of the man selected as from the percentage of the popular vote he wins. At the outset we must clearly establish and distinguish the end, the substantive object of the electoral process. The principle of majority or plurality vote in the selection of the President is not demeaned by a reminder that it is not the final cause or end of the electoral process. The end, inarguably, is to recruit, to select, to inaugurate men of the highest caliber, men most eminently qualified to lead the nation.

The consent of the governed is a necessary condition in leadership selection, but that consent is not always identical to the consent of the arithmetical majority of the voters. The people's choice is not necessarily the majority-vote victor, if only because not all the people vote. And though we are making great strides to remedy the situation, not all the people who wish to vote can. Moreover, the plurality winner is not even the first choice of the majority of the voters. This is not to deny the legitimacy inherent in the majority principle, but only to indicate that it is a device which, in practice, operates imperfectly, that at best we achieve an approximation of the principle which theoretically requires decisions to be made by 50 percent plus one of *all* the members. The implementation of the principle of majority rule in its absolute form is at the very least problematic, because it runs afoul of other goals such as noncompulsory voting, and because it depends on the existence of conditions in the actual or political world which do not always obtain, such as a high degree of consensus and an absence of incompatible alternatives. The answer to doctrinaire proponents of the majority principle is as it has always been: laws, including election laws, must be a compromise between wisdom and consent.

Except to a dogmatic majoritarian, the possibility of a runner-up President is not an unanswerable objection to the present system. But objections to a runner-up President are not on their face absurdly doctrinaire. A runner-up Presidency is formally an instance of minority rule, and substantively it could be a severe anomaly in a democratic regime. No one will argue that minority rule is in harmony with democracy. To the extent that runner-up presidencies are extreme and frequently occurring violations of majority rule they should not be countenanced. An extreme violation would be one in which the popular-vote margin between the candidates was large and the popular votes so distributed that the loser in the popular contest won in the electoral-vote contest. If, however, the popular-vote margin is small, the election approaches a standoff, particularly when the total electorate is large. Not every runner-up Presidency is a complete negation of the consent of the governed. It is absurd to cling tenaciously to the majority iple as the only valid rule of action in circumstances approach a standoff, if only because that rule does not nguish between the intensity of preferences. "The main practical conclusion is that the closer a group approaches to an equal division, the more any rule seems to be a mere matter of convenience."[7] In such a situation the best method may well be one that "the regime has incorporated through time and proven in practice."[8] Habit and custom are powerful stabilizing factors. As it works out in the partisan world, the present system has attached a federal-geographical rider to the rule of the majority. Despite this obvious break with the pure populistic theory, the possibility of a runner-up President may not be too great a price to pay for the requirement of a broadly based electoral victory.

In no case in our history has the electoral college rebuffed a man who had an undisputed majority of the popular vote. It is true that the record gives Tilden, the Democratic candidate in 1876, a popular-vote percentage of 50.93. In a number of states, however, the election could not be called a free one by any stretch of the imagination. In Florida, Louisiana, and South Carolina (to mention only three), corruption and intimidation were the watchwords of the electoral process. Fraud was practiced by both sides, but intimidation was the special forte of the Southern Democrats. There were riots, assassinations, murders, midnight raids by white rifle clubs that hunted Republican freedmen

7. Dahl, *Preface to Democratic Theory*, p. 41.
8. Myron Rush, *Political Succession in the USSR* (New York, 1965), p. 8.

through swamps and fields or shot them in their beds.[9] In one county—one example among a multitude—the white rifle club, in a raid on the Saturday night preceding the election, whipped six individuals and murdered two adults and a child.[10] In the casting, counting, and canvassing of votes there was every conceivable violation of the election laws. Paul Leland Haworth, in his detailed study of the disputed election, says of the elections in Florida and Louisiana:

Had there been a fair and free election in those states, there can be little if any doubt that the result in both would have been favorable to Hayes. If there had been a fair and free election throughout the South, there can be little question that Mississippi, with its great preponderance of blacks, and perhaps Alabama and North Carolina, would have ranged themselves in the Republican column, and that the much vaunted Democratic majority of the popular vote—which, after all, stood for absolutely nothing—would have been overcome.[11]

In our centennial year the electoral process was so debased and dishonored by fraud and intimidation that only an eccentric majoritarian would single out the technical runner-up Presidency of Hayes as a matter for criticism and concern.

Nor is Adams, the victor in the election of 1824, a good example of a runner-up President. Aside from the inconclusive status of the popular-vote contest and the atypical and varied means of selecting electors (mentioned in Chapter

9. Paul L. Haworth, *The Hayes-Tilden Disputed Presidential Election of 1876* (Cleveland, 1906).
10. *Ibid.*, p. 106.
11. *Ibid.*, pp. 340–341.

1, above), that election demonstrates the necessity for a national nominating convention to control access to candidacy. In 1824 there was a plethora of well-known and, except for William Crawford's health, able candidates. Henry Clay, Andrew Jackson (who, at first, was not considered a serious candidate), John Quincy Adams, and John C. Calhoun were nominated by state legislatures; Crawford was nominated by a discredited congressional caucus attended by fewer than one-third of the members. The number of candidates indicated to the political leaders that the election was almost certain to go to the House unless some way could be found to reduce that number. Both Adams and Jackson endorsed Calhoun for the Vice-Presidency, and the Crawford group attempted to bring Clay onto their ticket. But presidential ambition combined with the absence of a nominating convention served as a definitive point of no return for Clay. Perceiving that he had great strength in the House, Clay refused to combine forces. Clearly, he had little to lose and a great deal to gain by continuing his candidacy. Thus in 1824 there were four major candidates for the electoral votes, and they all were members of the Democratic-Republican party. The absence of a true opposition party meant there was little pressure for a conciliation of intraparty differences.

If anything, the election of 1824 indicates the necessity for a definite nomination process to sift and reduce candidacies. Presidential ambitions are not lightly abandoned, and if, as in Clay's case, there is reason for a candidate to believe he has a chance of victory or even an opportunity to increase his influence, he will continue in the contest.

The politicians of the time clearly perceived the problem, and in response, first the Jacksonians and later the Whigs adopted the national-convention system, originally introduced by the Antimasons in 1831.

The national-convention system has effectively controlled access to candidacy. In theory the mere existence of the House contingency procedure makes it possible for a disenchanted faction in a party to reject the party's candidate and run its own, but in practice this avenue is generally closed. With the universal adoption of the unit rule, the electoral system became a system of statewide pluralities. Unless a factional candidate can win statewide pluralities, he will not win any electoral votes. If he does not win electoral votes, he cannot prevent one of the two major-party candidates from obtaining the required majority of electoral votes, and the contingency procedure will not be invoked. The House decides the outcome of an election only if no candidate receives a majority of the electoral votes. A majority requirement is ordinarily a severe one, and given the principle of free access to inclusion on the ballot and the likelihood of two or three minor-party candidacies, the result would be a frequent use of the contingency procedure if the majority required were in popular votes. But it is not, and therein lies a world of difference.

Although the contingency election of John Q. Adams is not a clear and unequivocal example of a contest that resulted in a runner-up Presidency, the contingency election could produce one, since the House chooses among the top three candidates and is not required to select the candidate who leads in the popular vote. The probability of this is slight. In nine of the thirty-seven elections since 1824, a third or fourth candidate has polled more than 5 percent of the popular vote, and in ten a third or fourth candidate won electoral votes. Yet the nation has not had a single House election in 150 years. The reason for this is the fact that the unit system converts popular pluralities into electoral majorities, thus magnifying the margin of victory. (See Table 2.) In every election between 1832 and 1972, the state unit system converted popular statewide plurali-

Table 2. Direction of distortion in the relationship of popular to electoral vote (round numbers)*

Year	Winner Percentage		Year	Winner Percentage	
	Popular vote	Electoral vote		Popular vote	Electoral vote
1860	40	59	1908	52	66
1912	42	82	1840	53	80
1968	43	56	1868	53	73
1856	46	59	1944	53	81
1892	46	62	1924	54	71
1848	47	56	1832	55	77
1876	48	50	1864	55	91
1880	48	58	1940	55	85
1888	48	58	1952	55	83
1884	49	55	1872	56	82
1916	49	52	1904	56	71
1844	50	62	1932	57	89
1948	50	57	1956	57	86
1960	50	56	1928	58	84
1836	51	58	1920	60	76
1852	51	86	1936	61	98
1896	51	61	1964	61	90
1900	52	65	1972*	61	97

* Figures for 1972 are from the *Congressional Quarterly*, 30 (November 11, 1972), 2949.

ties into absolute electoral majorities. In 1876 and in 1888, the beneficiaries of this distortion between the popular and the electoral votes did not win the national popular plurality. In every case, nevertheless, this magnification produced a single election.

Defenders and critics of the present system have sometimes taken the wrong perspective on the phenomenon of distortion. Some defenders have suggested that the magnification makes for stability because it creates the impression of a mandate; critics have replied that this is sheer nonsense, that the electorate is not hoodwinked by such an artificial ploy. But its value (as Table 2 indicates) seems to be twofold: (1) it makes electoral-vote majorities the rule, effectively foreclosing the probability of contingency elections and thereby the possibility of the House selecting a President who is the runner-up in the popular contest; (2) in every election but one it has worked to the advantage of the undisputed plurality victor, thus radically limiting the possibility of the electoral college itself producing a runner-up President.

Neal Peirce disagrees, and argues that despite the magnification of the winner's margin of victory in the electoral count, only sheer luck has saved the nation from a series of runner-up presidencies.[12] My contention, however, is that it is not sheer luck but rather the plurality basis of the electoral-count system and the power-preoccupation of the

12. *The People's President: The Electoral College in American History and the Direct Vote Alternative* (New York, 1968), p. 141. See also Harvey Zeidenstein, *Direct Election of the President* (Lexington, Mass., 1973), pp. 8–9.

political parties. The electoral-count system is essentially a plurality system: to win a state's electoral votes a party need not win a majority of the votes within the state but only a plurality. No rewards, no extra electoral votes are given to the candidate who amasses a huge margin of victory in any state or states. As a result, candidates and campaign managers pay little attention to their so-called sure states. Increasing the expenditure of campaign resources in their sure states would only increase an already sufficient statewide margin of victory. If a candidate's popular appeal is intensely concentrated in a few states it would, of course, increase his popular-vote total but not his electoral-vote total. Thus there is a point where geographic concentration of votes is unproductive. Therefore the parties work to broaden their candidate's appeal. Although each party historically has had a regional or sectional base of sure states, these have not been sufficient. So the parties endeavor to move out of their home territories; they are encouraged to concentrate their efforts in the competitive states and roused to make inroads on the less secure territory of the opposition. A party that does not do so will lose, because the votes it wins will not be properly distributed. In this light, a runner-up Presidency is as much the fault of the losing party as of the electoral-count system.

With this in mind, we must consider in some detail the direction of the distortion of the popular vote by the electoral-count system, with particular reference to the exception which proves the rule, the only undisputed case of a runner-up Presidency. Though the magnification of the popular-vote winner's margin of victory is not an ironclad guarantee, it may be far more reliable than the critics admit. Most critics, including Peirce, suggest that the dangers of misfire are immediate in any close election. Congressman Celler suggests that we must not "continue the risk of electing a candidate who was the popular loser, a risk . . . which apparently increases the closer the popular election results become."[13]

Although a close election contest is one factor that limits the tendency to inflate the winner's margin, it is not the only one, nor perhaps the sufficient one. Table 3, which

Table 3. Disparity between popular and electoral vote in close elections (in percent)

| Year* | Popular margin between candidates | Plurality winner | | Disparity |
		Popular vote	Electoral vote	
1880	.1	48.3	57.9	9.6
1884	.2	48.5	54.5	6.0
1960	.2	49.7	56.4	6.7
1968	.7	43.4	55.9	12.5
1888	.8	48.6	41.8	—6.8
1844	1.5	49.5	61.8	12.3
1892	3.0	46.0	62.3	16.3
1916	3.1	49.2	52.1	2.9
1896	4.2	51.0	60.6	9.6
1948	4.5	49.5	57.0	7.5
1848	4.8	47.3	56.2	8.9
1900	6.1	51.6	65.3	13.7
1856	12.3	45.6	58.7	13.1
1836	14.3	50.9	57.7	6.8

* The election of 1876 is not included because of the unusual circumstances affecting it, particularly the fraudulent practices investigated by the Electoral Commission.

13. *Congressional Record*, Vol. 115, Pt. 19, 91st Cong., 1st sess. (1969), p. 25165.

ranks elections according to the popular margins between the candidates, shows that in the close elections in our history there is no direct correlation between the closeness of the popular contest and the tendency to magnify the popular winner's margin of victory.

The election of 1888, which did produce a runner-up President, Benjamin Harrison, was indeed an extremely close one. But the election of 1916, which came nearest to repeating the situation, ranks eighth in the category of close elections; Woodrow Wilson's margin over Charles Evans Hughes was 3.1 percent. In the elections of 1884, 1948, and 1836, in which the disparity between the popular and the electoral votes was also small, the margin between the major candidates ranges from 0.2, to 4.5, to 14.3 percent. It would seem that some other factor or factors must be functioning, for the disparity between the popular and electoral votes does not decrease as the popular margin between the candidates decreases.

The election of 1880 was the closest election in our history in terms of popular votes. James Garfield won by a margin of .1 percent of the popular votes, by 9,457 votes. Yet this insignificant popular margin was converted by the electoral count system into 214 electoral votes, 29 more than necessary. Svend Petersen gives statistics showing how a shift of 10,517 votes in New York would have given Hancock the election.[14] But it would also have given him the popular plurality. In this closest of all elections to date, the tendency of the electoral-count system to inflate a win-

14. Petersen, *Statistical History*, p. 48.

ner's margin of victory functioned quite adequately, and Garfield won with 57.9 percent of the electoral vote.

In 1880, Garfield, a former member of the Electoral Commission of 1877, was a compromise candidate of the Republican party chosen on the thirty-sixth ballot. Hancock won his nomination by default. The honesty of the Hayes administration prevented a bolt by reform Republicans, and Hayes's withdrawal of federal troops that had supported the carpetbag Republican governments in the South made possible the South's transformation into a Democratic stronghold. Edward Stanwood attributes Garfield's insignificant plurality to the "abstention voluntary and enforced, on the part of Republican voters in the South."[15]

If an extremely close election is not in itself sufficient to overcome a distortion tendency favorable to the plurality victor, what is? Among the other possible factors, the most decisive may be the distribution of the popular votes. In a close popular election, the tendency of the electoral-count system to inflate the popular-vote winner's margin depends on the distribution of the popular votes. If his votes are efficiently distributed—that is, if he wins a fair percentage of the electoral votes by narrow popular margins and wastes few of his popular votes in landslide victories—the electoral-count system will inflate his margin of victory. Conversely, in a close election if the popular-vote loser's votes are efficiently distributed, the tendency of the electoral-count system is to deflate the popular-vote winner's margin

15. *A History of the Presidency* (Boston, 1898), p. 418.

of victory. Table 4 gives the figures for the vote-distribution patterns in the close elections.

Electoral votes are won in state-sized lots; under the unit

Table 4. Vote distribution in close elections (in percent)

Year	Pop.-vote margin between candidates	Disparity between pop.-vote winner's electoral and pop. votes	Narrow wins[†] (in % of majority of electoral votes)		Landslides[†] (in % of majority of electoral votes)	
			Pop. winner	Pop. loser	Pop. winner	Pop. loser
1880	.1	9.6	32	7	13	28
1884	.2	6.0	38	0	26	1
1960	.2	6.7	60	17	11	5
1968*	.7	12.5	45	16	0	7
1888	.8	−6.8	20	53	31	1
1844	1.5	12.3	60	33	2	0
1892*	3.0	16.3	19	13	13	1
1916	3.1	2.9	8	15	40	1
1896	4.2	9.6	10	3	31	35
1948	4.5	7.5	34	36	20	1
1848*	4.8	8.9	6	27	2	2
1900	6.1	13.7	1	5	29	35
1856*	12.3	13.1	0	0	11	17
1836*	14.3	6.8	28	5	13	0

* Years when a third or fourth candidate had a large popular following.
† Narrow wins are defined as those with a margin of 3 percent or less; landslides as wins of 60 percent of the vote or more.

rule the winner of a plurality of popular votes in a state wins 100 percent of that state's electoral votes. Table 4 analyzes these state-sized victories in terms of the margin of victory *in each state*. Therefore, if a candidate wins New York with 60 percent of the popular vote (or more), he has won New York's electoral votes by a landslide (as defined in the table). If a candidate wins New Jersey with a popular-vote margin of 3 percent (or less) he wins all of New Jersey's electoral votes narrowly (as defined in the table). The popular-vote winner's and loser's percentages of landslides and narrow wins are determined by converting the total number of electoral votes won by each candidate in state landslides and narrow wins to percentages of the majority of electoral votes (the number needed to win in the electoral college). The table compares the national popular-vote winner's percentage of the majority of electoral votes in landslides and narrow wins to the national popular-vote loser's percentages in order to demonstrate the effect of the distribution of popular votes on the distortion between popular- and electoral-vote percentages. In short, winning a state's electoral votes by a popular landslide *within that state* results in a dysfunctional distribution of popular votes under the electoral-college system.

In 1916, when Wilson polled a 3.1 percent popular margin over Hughes, the disparity between his popular- and electoral-vote percentages was only 2.9 percent, and he won with only 52.1 percent of the electoral vote. On the other hand, in 1892, when Grover Cleveland polled a 3 percent popular margin over Harrison, the disparity between Cleveland's popular- and electoral-vote percentages was 16.3, and he won with 62.3 percent of the electoral vote. In 1916, however, Wilson's vote distribution was remarkably inefficient. He wasted more of his votes in landslide victories than any other candidate in a close election, and he won fewer electoral votes by narrow margins than did his opponent. In 1892, Cleveland's distribution, though not a model of efficiency, was significantly better than Wilson's. Cleveland won more narrow victories than his opponent and only 13 percent of the majority of electoral votes by landslides.

In both 1884 and 1960, two of the closest elections in our history, the popular margins between the two major candidates were 0.2 percent. In 1884 the disparity between Cleveland's popular and electoral votes was 6 percent; in 1960 the disparity between John Kennedy's popular and electoral votes was 6.7 percent. Kennedy won the election with 56.4 percent of the electoral votes, and Cleveland won with 55 percent. Both candidates achieved an efficient vote-distribution pattern. Kennedy won 60 percent of the majority of electoral votes with narrow victories and wasted only 11 percent in landslides. Although Cleveland wasted 26 percent of the majority of electoral votes in landslides, he captured the entire narrow-victory category with 38 percent. When a plurality candidate achieves an efficient vote-distribution pattern, when he wins a greater percentage of the majority of electoral votes by narrow margins than by landslides, his electoral-vote percentage will be significantly inflated even if his popular plurality is as little as 0.2 percent. Furthermore, the popular-to-electoral-vote distortion is favorable to the plurality victor as long as he beats his opponent in the vote-distribution contest. In 1896, 1900, and 1856, the popular winners wasted a high percentage of their votes in landslides, but their electoral-vote percentages were nonetheless inflated, since their vote-distribution patterns were more efficient than their opponents'.

Contrary to the critics' fears, the dangers of misfire are demonstrably not immediate in any and every close election. The electoral-count system, as demonstrated in actual practice, inflates the plurality winner's margin of victory unless his votes are distributed uneconomically. To put it in the terms of American politics, it would appear that misfire is likely only when a close election coincides with a sectionally imbalanced candidacy or campaign.

The election of 1888, the year of the runner-up President, presents a remarkable vote-distribution pattern, a veritable model of frugality by the popular-vote loser Harrison. He won 53 percent of the majority of electoral votes by narrow margins and wasted few of his votes on landslides. His opponent, Cleveland, the popular-vote victor, wasted a high percentage of his popular votes in landslide victories. The combination of a close election, an extremely efficient vote-distribution pattern by the popular-vote loser, and an inefficient vote-distribution pattern by the popular-vote winner produced a runner-up President. Harrison's economy was matched by Cleveland's prodigality.

In no other close contest did the runner-up achieve such an extremely high percentage of narrow victories. In 1948, Thomas Dewey managed to register 36 percent, but Harry Truman came very close to matching him, with 34 percent. In 1844, Henry Clay achieved 33 percent, but James Polk clearly outclassed him, with 60 percent. In 1848, Lewis Cass attained 27 percent in narrow victories, but Zachary Taylor did not exhaust any significant amount of his 4.8 percent margin in landslide victories. Only in 1916, when Charles Hughes won twice as many electoral votes by narrow margins, and Wilson hit the high mark in land-slides, did the combination of thrift and wastefulness recur, and we came very close to having another runner-up President. The vote-distribution pattern of 1888 is, then, atypical and unlikely to recur frequently, given the wit and ingenuity of the political parties.

An inefficient or uneconomic vote-distribution pattern is associated with a sectional candidate or campaign. As Sayre and Parris point out, "One party states are thus the major contributors to any discrepancy between the results of the popular vote and those of the electoral vote."[16] It is a fact of American political history that there have been severe sectional divisions in this nation, but we have had only one runner-up Presidency. The electoral-count system discriminates against sectional candidates and campaigns. Sectional candidacies are the product of the world of politics, and in that world political parties have a decisive role to play.

According to James MacGregor Burns, the parties have performed their task admirably. He goes so far as to claim that "the historic achievement of the presidential party" has been "the immense widening of the electorate." The reason is that the presidential candidates have the incentive "to widen and 'flatten out' their vote, to win states by dependable but not wasteful popular majorities, while the congressional party 'bunches' its vote in safe districts."[17]

16. Wallace S. Sayre and Judith H. Parris, *Voting for President: The Electoral College and the American Political System* (Washington, 1972), p. 59.

17. James MacGregor Burns, *The Deadlock of Democracy* (Englewood Cliffs, N.J., 1965), p. 251.

The incentive is provided by the electoral-count system; the 1880 election is an exception which proves the rule.

To the extent that one-party states are major contributors to the risk of a runner-up Presidency, that risk has diminished considerably. According to the calculations of Sayre and Parris, there were 16 one-party states in 1880, but only 12 in 1960. The one-party states, in 1880, possessed 34.4 percent of the electoral votes, as contrasted with only 16.8 percent in 1960. In 1880, one-party states cast 17.6 percent of the popular votes, whereas they cast only 8.3 percent in 1960.[18] The one-party-state phenomenon is declining, and the decline, combined with the "historic achievement" of the political parties, means that a runner-up President will be rare indeed.

Harrison's runner-up Presidency was not the result of unlucky chance (chance and accident are factors in any election) as much as of some unusual and improvident political decisions. As with most elections, the contest in 1888 was a complicated affair, a tangle of many factors. But if we were to single out one, it would be the fact that Cleveland's votes were not properly distributed. His appeal was intensely and improvidently concentrated.

The elections following the reconstruction period were sectional contests; the Democrats had a firm hold on the South, and the Republicans a sufficient hold on the North and West to win without any southern states. The southern electoral-vote total was only 153, while the northern total was 248; 201 were necessary for victory. A Democratic

18. Sayre and Parris, *Voting for President*, p. 60.

candidate needed 48 northern electoral votes. Since New York possessed 36 electoral votes and was a competitive state, it was generally a crucial state in any campaign.

Neal Peirce asserts that single states dictated the results in the elections of the 1880's.[19] They did so only in a qualified sense, since New York alone would not have given the victory to the Democrats, and, moreover, the Republicans conceivably could have won without it. More correctly the elections turned on the results in the four competitive states, New York, New Jersey, Connecticut, and Indiana. In 1888 the Democrats won only two of these states, Connecticut and New Jersey, with a total of 15 electoral votes.

A study of the state-by-state returns indicates the degree to which the election of 1888 was a sectional contest. Cleveland's popular-vote percentages were extremely high in the deep South (his highest was 82.73 in South Carolina); they decreased in the border states to percentages in the middle fifties. Harrison's highest percentages were in New England and decreased farther south. While the North, except for the four key states, could be characterized as Republican, it was by no means as solid as the South was for the Democrats. Cleveland, the Democratic contender, won 61 electoral votes in six states with margins of 35 percent or more. Harrison, the Republican, won only 13 electoral votes with margins of 20 percent or more. Harrison's popular support was evenly distributed; Cleveland's was concentrated.

In 1880 and 1884 the votes had also been cast in sectional

19. *People's President*, p. 92.

patterns, but among the factors distinguishing the election of 1888 from the previous two was the greater solidity of the deep South in 1888. A comparable increase had not occurred in the Republican North. Six states—Alabama, Florida, Georgia, Louisiana, Mississippi, and South Carolina—augmented their already large Democratic margins by percentages ranging from 5 to 17; the average increase was 9 percent. This increase in Democratic votes in the solid South is easily explained. In 1887, Cleveland, in his annual message to the Congress, made a plea for tariff revision. The tariff, which favored the industries of the Northeast and was in sharp conflict with the agrarian interests of the South, was a highly partisan and sectional issue of long standing. Cleveland, as the incumbent, was in a position to shape the issues of the approaching election. He and his party needed to make inroads into the Republican strength in the North, especially in the four key states. But his decision to push for tariff reform could only, and did indeed, result in undermining Republican strength in the South, which he clearly did not need to do.[20] The Republicans were jubilant; backed by the money of aroused Northern industrial giants, they believed, correctly, that they could hold onto the North.

Furthermore, in making a plea for tariff revision, Cleveland, who owed his election in 1884 quite as much to the dissident, reformist Republicans as to his own party, forced

20. In four of the six states of the deep South the turnout and the Democratic total were substantially increased; in the remaining two the turnout and the Republican total were substantially reduced.

on the campaign a highly partisan issue that was bound to overshadow all other political questions. In so doing, he very probably lost the election. Stanwood, generally moderate in his conclusions, calls this act unusual and startling.[21] With the support of the independent Republicans, Cleveland's party had won the Presidency in 1884 for the first time in twenty-four years, yet in 1888 he raised a partisan issue in the campaign. His party's sectional base was insufficient for victory, yet he raised a sectional issue. Cleveland lost this election because his votes were not properly distributed; his votes were not properly distributed because of his improvident political decision to force the tariff issue. The Democratic politicians of the time held the same view.[22]

The republic's only undisputed runner-up President, Benjamin Harrison, won because his opponent, Grover Cleveland, ran a sectional campaign. The electoral-count system discriminates against candidates who rely too heavily on a sectional base. Consequently, it is the electoral-count system that provides the presidential parties with the incentive "to widen and 'flatten out' their vote." James MacGregor Burns is correct in claiming that the historic achievement of the presidential parties has been just this. But would they have done so if the electoral-count system had not made it necessary for victory?

Despite the fact that we have had but one true runner-up President and only two hairbreadth electoral-vote contests (in 1876, when Hayes won a bare 50 percent of the elec-

21. *Presidential Elections,* p. 458.
22. *Ibid.,* p. 492.

toral vote, and in 1916, when Wilson won 52 percent), several opponents of the electoral-count system believe we have come much too close to electing the wrong man in many elections. These critics argue that a strategically placed shift in the popular vote could have produced a runner-up President or a deadlock in the electoral college. In the 1969 House hearings, William T. Gossett, president of the American Bar Association, testified that "in 15 elections a shift of less than 1 percent of the national vote would have made the popular vote loser President."[23] Congressmen Emanuel Celler and William McCulloch agreed with this conclusion.[24] Gossett asserted, in addition, that in seven elections, including those of 1948, 1960, and 1968, "a shift of less than 1 percent of the popular vote in a few key states would have thrown those elections into Congress, with the consequent risk of political deals and possibly the election of a President who was rejected by a majority of the voters."[25] James C. Kirby has made the same argument about the election of 1960.[26]

By and large this argument miscarries if only because it abstracts from political realities. The electorate does cast its votes in statewide separate constituencies, but as every candidate knows, the states are not soundproof rooms wherein

23. U.S., House of Representatives, Committee on the Judiciary, *Hearings, Electoral College Reform*, 91st Cong., 1st sess., 1969, p. 176 (cited hereafter as 1969 House *Hearings*).

24. *Congressional Record*, Vol. 115, Pt. 19, 91st Cong., 1st sess. (1969), pp. 24963, 24967.

25. 1969 House *Hearings*, p. 176.

26. "Turmoil on the Electoral College Campus," *The Progressive* 32 (Oct. 1968), 13–17.

a candidate can make special pleas that will not be heard in other states. In most of these fifteen elections any appeals that would cause such strategic shifts would have wide-ranging effects and would no doubt reverse the national popular tally. And, as we have argued earlier, the state unit system has magnified the undisputed national plurality winner's margin of victory in every election save one. The possibility of a runner-up President is stronger in theory than in reality. The unit rule has persistently reinforced the results of the popular election.

Because the shift-in-votes argument was used in 1969 by some of the leading opponents of the present system, particularly by the ABA and by the chairman of the House Judiciary Committee and by its ranking member, it may be useful to examine the argument in some detail. The election of 1844 is one of the fifteen elections in which it is claimed that a shift of less than 1 percent of the national vote would have produced a runner-up President. Svend Petersen claims that in 1844 "a switch of 2,555 votes out of the 2,640,055 cast for Polk and Clay—.097%" would have made the latter a runner-up President.[27] Since the shift of 2,555 votes had to occur in one state, New York, the actual shift required was 0.54 percent. In abstract mathematical terms, the conclusion about a Clay victory is correct. To the extent, however, that this argument abstracts from the political realities of the time, it fails.

In 1844 the salient issues were expansion and the annexation of Texas. Prior to the conventions, Henry Clay, who seemed assured of the Whig nomination, and Martin Van

27. *Statistical History*, p. 26.

Buren of the Democratic one, both wrote letters indicating their positions on the Texas question. This was necessary because the incumbent, President John Tyler, had sent the treaty of annexation to the Senate in April 1844. The issue of slavery was intertwined with the annexation question, and Van Buren's opposition to annexation probably cost him the Democratic nomination. James Polk, who won it instead, took a nationalist stand on annexation and in the election confronted Clay, whose preconvention letter had also opposed annexation. A third party, the abolitionist Liberty party, further complicated matters for Clay. He was neatly checkmated on the Texas question, for he could either alienate the South by holding firm to his original position or alienate the northern abolitionists by modifying that position.

If Clay had won New York, all other things remaining the same, he would have been a runner-up President. But what would have caused a shift in New York votes? Some political act, some campaign factor should account for such a shift, unless votes are cast randomly or arbitrarily. If, for example, Clay had not softened his position on annexation—an act which so angered the abolitionists that James Birney, leader of the Liberty party, openly advised his followers to vote for Polk—he might have increased his following in the North and sufficiently in New York to win that state. We cannot argue, however, that this would have given him the election, for political acts cannot be isolated and considered only in relationship to the areas where they will prove beneficial. As Eugene Roseboom points out, "His concessions to southern sentiments on Texas possibly tilted the balance to him in Tennessee. His margin there was only 113 votes. Defeat in Tennessee even with victory in New York would have lost him the election."[28]

By proposing minor and imaginary shifts in the popular votes between the two leading candidates in fifteen close elections, the critics suggest that the electoral-count system can easily and frequently produce a runner-up President. Many elections have been characterized by highly significant shifts in voting patterns, but there are reasons, political acts, behind these shifts, and their effects are not confined to an individual state or even to key states. But in a close election, unless the proposed shifts are in fact limited to the key states, the reversal of the electoral contest usually will not produce a runner-up President. In 1884, when the national popular-vote margin between the two candidates was 0.2 percent, a shift of .05 percent in one state, New York, would have made Blaine a runner-up President. Unless that seemingly minor shift was in fact limited to New York, Blaine would have been a plurality President. It is highly unlikely that such shifts would be limited to fit the predictions of the critics, as the election of 1884 demonstrates.

In 1884 numerous vote shifts from the Republicans to both the Democratic and Prohibition party candidates cost the Republican candidate the election and, of course, significantly affected the national popular-vote tally. The primary reason for the swing away from the Repeublicans was the Mugwump movement. Prior to and during the cam-

28. Eugene Roseboom, *A Short History of Presidential Elections* (New York, 1967), p. 60.

paign a strong sentiment against "machine" politics and bossism had developed. The Republican candidate, James Blaine, was associated, in the minds of the reformist faction of the Republican party, with political corruption and the era of plunder. After his nomination the independent Republicans, the Mugwumps, bolted the party and made overtures to the Democrats, who selected Cleveland as a nominee acceptable to the reformers. Cleveland, whose reputation for integrity was his most valuable asset in obtaining the nomination, ran under the slogan "A Public Office Is a Public Trust."

In this election the key states were Connecticut, Indiana, New York, and New Jersey. Cleveland, with the solid South behind him, needed only 48 electoral votes in the North to win. He won all four key states—New York by only 0.1 percent. In these states the reformers held the balance of power, and they voted either for Cleveland or for John St. John, a former Republican governor of Kansas, who was running as the Prohibition candidate. The disaffection of the reformers is clearly evidenced by the strong showing of St. John. In all four key states St. John's votes apparently cut severely into the Republican strength, as the following percentages indicate.

	Prohibition votes		Democratic plurality
State	1880	1884	1884
Conn.	.31	1.82	.94
Ind.	0	.61	1.31
N.J.	.08	2.36	1.67
N.Y.	.14	2.4	.10

Although a number of factors helped the Democrats in New York, among them the "Rum, Romanism and Rebellion" blunder, the opposition of Tammany, and a rainstorm in upstate New York, the crucial and determinative factor in the election was the Mugwump movement. This movement also cost Blaine many votes in states which he won, such as Massachusetts. Roseboom argues convincingly that the reform movement was the fundamental factor. "The reform groups held the balance of power in the four northern states carried by Cleveland and reduced the Republican vote in other states. But for their activity in New York, Blaine would have won by such a margin that preacher, prohibitionist and rainstorm combined could not have changed the result."[29]

As for Petersen's suggestion that a shift of 575 votes in New York would have made Blaine a runner-up President,[30] it is possible that the Romanism blunder disaffected enough of the Irish vote to cut into Blaine's strength. It is also possible that the rainstorm tipped the scales against the Republicans (assuming that a sufficient number of voters— 1,150—were deterred from voting and would have voted for Blaine instead of St. John). To base conclusions on such possibilities is to view the election from a narrow perspective, to disregard the total political situation and, in particular, the effectiveness of the Mugwump movement. After the Hayes administration had returned home rule to the South, the Republican vote there was greatly reduced; consequently, the party had to rely on the North. Thus the

29. *Ibid.*, p. 119.
30. *Statistical History*, p. 51.

party could ill afford any dissension in its ranks. The Republicans had been given a warning in 1882, when they suffered numerous defeats, that if they did not adopt a reform candidate they would lose the election. Viewed from a broad perspective, the election turned on the Republican failure of foresight. Both Stanwood and Roseboom suggest that in selecting Blaine as their candidate, the Republicans voluntarily accepted such a stringent handicap that the election was a tossup.

In this election there was no popular majority; the margin between the major candidates was .24 percent; and 3.4 percent of the voting population were unwilling to support either of them. Many Republicans opposed Blaine with such intensity that they bolted their party yet could not bring themselves to vote for Cleveland. It is difficult to determine the popular will regarding the two major candidates and therefore difficult to prove that if Blaine had won New York and become a runner-up President, the result would have been a serious violation of democratic principles. As Robert Dahl suggests in his analysis of the populistic theory, "The closer a group approaches to an equal division the less valid the majority principle becomes."[31] In 1888, only 23,737 votes separated the two front runners. Only a doctrinaire dedication to the principle of majority rule will suffice to support the argument that a Blaine victory would have been unsuitable for a democratic nation, or a complete negation of the concept of the consent of the governed.

31. *Preface to Democratic Theory*, p. 41.

In the elections of 1844 and 1884, it is claimed, a minor shift in a single state, New York, could have produced a runner-up President. But in many of the fifteen close elections cited by the critics, a shift of votes in as many as eight states would have been required. It is argued that only small shifts would have been needed, less than 1 percent of the national vote. Close examination of the figures indicates that, more often than not, major shifts would have been required in a few key states. The necessary shifts appear to be minor only if the election laws are ignored. The election of 1856 demonstrates this point.

In the election of 1856, the year of the first Republican candidacy, there were three strong candidates. The Whigs were fielding their last candidate, Millard Fillmore. The Republicans were an openly sectional party. Their candidate, John C. Frémont, did not appear on the ballot in the South. Petersen suggests that a shift of 17,427 votes from James Buchanan, the Democratic nominee, to Frémont in Indiana and Illinois and from Buchanan to Fillmore in Delaware would have thrown the election into the House.[32] Petersen converts such strategic shifts into national vote percentages. In this case the shift in terms of the national vote was .43 percent. But this percentage is highly misleading, for elections are not decided by an across-the-board national vote and if they were, a shift of .43 percent would not have resulted in a deadlock or deprived Buchanan of the Presidency. Buchanan's margin over Frémont in Indiana was 10.7 percent, and in Delaware Buchanan led Fillmore by a margin of 12.6 percent.

32. *Statistical History*, p. 33.

Neal Peirce, who does not follow Petersen's lead, also gives figures which may be misleading. Instead of computing the shift required in percentages of the national vote, he treats the three states as a unit and gives a combined figure for the three states that would have been involved in the necessary shift. Thus he claims that in 1856 "a shift of 3.554 percent in the three crucial states alone" would have created a deadlock.[33] But the three states are not a unit under the electoral-count system. The actual shift required was 5 percent in Indiana, 2 percent in Illinois, and 6 percent in Delaware. A shift of 6 percent in Delaware or of 5 percent in Indiana might well have been more difficult to achieve than a 3.5 percent shift in all three states and even more difficult than a .43 percent shift in the nation. In 1856, despite three serious candidacies and a three-way division of the electoral vote, the unit rule converted Buchanan's popular plurality into 58.7 percent of the electoral vote, for an increase of 13 percent over his popular percentage.

The shift-in-votes argument fails to prove that the electoral-count system can easily and frequently produce a runner-up President or an electoral-college deadlock. It fails because it abstracts from political realities and because in many cases it ignores the election laws. The present system can produce a runner-up President; but the historical evidence indicates that it will do so only in a close election in which the plurality candidate's vote is inefficiently distributed. Since the system penalizes candidates who rely on

33. Peirce, *People's President*, p. 319.

their popular strength in one-party states to give them the popular plurality, the political parties attempt to broaden their candidates' appeal. This unanticipated benefit is ignored by the critics.

There is a risk in our electoral-count system, and that risk is the possibility of a runner-up President. While the evidence cited in this chapter would suggest that the plurality victor has little cause for concern because of the tendency of the system to inflate his margin of victory in the electoral college, the possibility of a runner-up President cannot be denied. The majority principle is in truth one of the basic tenets of our system, and we may not lightly pass over the possibility of thwarting it. On the other hand, the majority principle is not the only principle underlying our republic. There are other goals such as minority consent, two-partyism, pluralism, and stability. There is the governmental structure as a whole, which manifestly is not in complete harmony with the majority principle. There is the world of practical consequences. In practice, the system has not discriminated against a durable and determined majority. When, as in 1824 and 1888, the plurality candidate was passed over, the distortion was soon corrected. In 1828, Jackson was elected, and in 1892, Cleveland. And the system has recruited distinguished men of exceptional caliber and ability. In 1876 and in 1916, when we came very close to electing runner-up presidents, the major contestants were able and eminent men; the election of any of them would not have been a major disaster for the Presidency.

In the congressional hearings and debate, it became apparent that one goal of the reformers is to bring the influence of all the states into the presidential election. Senator Bayh phrased this concern in the following terms:

As a result of the mysterious arithmetic of the present system, for example, a candidate could win an electoral majority by capturing popular vote pluralities—no matter how small—in only eleven of the largest states and the District of Columbia. In short, the voters of thirty-nine states would have absolutely no voice in the choice of a President, even if they were unanimous in their opposition.[34]

Theoretically, this is true; however, it is implausible to the point of fantasy. But underlying this example, we may detect a concern not only for a plurality President, but also for a President who represents the nation in its diversity, who owes his victory to broad nationwide support and not to blocs of homogeneous, safe states. It is important to remember that it is not populous states per se that are favored under the present system but populous pivotal states. A populous state that is a one-party state may also be neglected by both parties.

In 1970, Senator Thomas Eagleton, who would require a broad-based victory, submitted a plan which "would require a popular vote winner to carry either a majority of the states or a plurality of the vote in any group of states casting more than 50 percent of the total vote."[35] Tom Wicker, who has been a vocal proponent of direct election, found this proposal "fairer than some of the other proposals

34. Birch Bayh, "Comment," *Villanova Law Review* 13 (Winter 1968), p. 333.
35. *New York Times*, April 19, 1970, p. 17.

now before the Senate Judiciary Committee."[36] It is interesting to note that Harrison, the only runner-up President, would have passed both of Eagleton's tests, and he carried twenty of the thirty-eight states.

Our electoral system is not neutral; it discriminates against the homogeneous sectors, the one-party states. Perhaps the American people are better served by a system that does not allow lopsided sectional majorities to dominate the presidential contest. Perhaps the people are better served by the creation of political majorities that are cross sections, not sections, of the nation.

36. *Ibid.*

3 The Contingency Election

All the objections raised against the present contingency-election procedure are undermined by the fact that for almost 150 years the presidential contests have been resolved in the general elections. Since its universal adoption, the unit system has made electoral-vote majorities the rule. Thus contingency elections have been unnecessary. Nevertheless, because a contingency election is possible and because there is widespread agreement that the contingency procedure should be changed, there has been no shortage of proposed reforms.

Many defects of the present contingency procedure, including the injustice of giving each state one vote in the House and of depriving a state of its vote when its delegation is tied, as well as the possibility of a President and a Vice-President of different parties, can be corrected without resorting to radical electoral surgery. Among the many proposals is a plan for a runoff between the two leading candidates if no candidate receives a majority of the electoral vote, offered by Congressman Jonathan Bingham.[1]

1. U.S., House of Representatives, Committee on the Judiciary, *Hearings, Electoral College Reform*, 91st Cong., 1st sess., 1969, p. 57 (cited hereafter as 1969 House *Hearings*).

Congressman Hale Boggs has proposed an alternative: a runoff if no candidate receives 40 percent of the electoral vote. It is significant that both these contingency proposals retain the electoral-count system though not the electors.

Another proposal, perhaps the most popular among those who would retain the electoral-count system, would give the decision to a joint session of Congress, with each member having one vote. Supporters maintain that the joint-session plan has the advantages of the existing system without all of its defects. Retention of the electoral-count system makes resort to this contingency plan remote. On the other hand, giving the decision to a joint session rather than to the House voting by states would mean that the President and Vice-President would be of the same party, no state would lose its vote, and the more populous states would have fairer representation in the decision-making process. The supporters point out that whenever the general election fails to produce a winner there has been a failure in the coalition-building process. A new attempt must therefore be made. Alexander Bickel argues that "coalition-making is a function of a representative, deliberative institution" and that therefore "Congress sitting in joint session and reaching decisions by a majority of individual votes of its members is the best available deliberative institution for this purpose at such a time."[2] If a coalition is not made by a formal existing body, such as a national convention or the Congress, it must and will be made by the candidates and their representatives. In this sense, deals and trades cannot be avoided once a general election fails. Some

2. *The New Age of Political Reform* (New York, 1968), p. 20.

political leaders, therefore, agree with Congressman Lawrence Coughlin, who would prefer to have the "question decided by 535 members from both our major parties than by three or four or five candidates wheeling and dealing among themselves."[3] If trades and deals cannot be avoided once the general election fails, there is something to be said for entrusting the coalition-building process to the people's elected representatives, who have a long-term interest in public office.

Several objections have been raised against the joint-session plan. First, it would violate the separation-of-powers principle. Since the founders who introduced this principle into our Constitution did not believe it would be imperiled by their contingency election in the House, perhaps those concerned about the separation of powers are too fastidious. Another objection is that it would still allow the candidate who did not win the plurality to be selected. The winner of the popular plurality could lose if he belonged to the congressional minority party. Since 1948, the Democrats have controlled both the House and the Senate in every presidential election year except 1952. During this time the Republicans have won the Presidency four times and the Democrats only twice. If we assume a straight partisan division, except in the 1952 election, a Republican candidate could not have won in the House either under the existing contingency system of voting by states or under the joint-session plan. In 1968, an election by a joint session would have yielded 301 votes for the Democratic candidate

3. *Congressional Record*, Vol. 115, Pt. 19, 91st Cong., 1st sess. (1969), p. 25981.

and 234 for the Republican. Under the existing system, in 1968, the result would have been 21 Democratic states, 5 Democratic states that had voted for Wallace, 19 Republican states, and 5 states tied and therefore unable to vote. The Democrats could have won in the House if the 5 Democratic Wallace states had voted with them. But the Republicans could not have won even if the Wallace states had joined them, because according to the Constitution "a majority of all states shall be necessary to a choice." If one believes the polls and the suggestions of the political analysts, most Wallace voters preferred Nixon to Humphrey, yet a Nixon-Wallace coalition alone could not have won in the House under its existing rules. Under either the present or the joint-session contingency system the only way the candidate of the congressional minority party can win is if there is not a straight partisan vote.

Although it is dangerous to assume that all congressmen would vote for the candidate of their party, partisan pressures would be at their greatest when the election of a President was at stake. Within the Congress itself, partisan loyalty is at its peak during the process of organizing each house and selecting the leadership. On the other hand, the members would be subject to a series of pressures, such as those arising from the orientation of their constituencies. If a member's district or state had gone over to the other party he might feel pressured to act as its delegate and cross party lines. Others might cross party lines on principle, believing they should vote for the plurality winner regardless of party. Some members, such as those from the Wallace states, might vote for the congressional minority party's candidate out of conviction or as the lesser of two evils. The very existence of such cross-pressures could be used as the basis for demanding policy concessions or favors from either candidate. Such cross-pressures would provide a congressman with a rationale for explaining or excusing his vote. The Presidency is the greatest prize a political party can win, and it would be dangerous to discount the pull of partisan loyalty, but if there was not a straight partisan vote, backroom deals could blossom in the Congress. It would be naïve to expect that independents and those who would cross party lines would not exact promises or expect favors in return for their votes. Giving the decision to either a joint session or to the House would place tremendous burdens on Congress that in such a partisan body could prove to be severely dysfunctional. The bitterness, hostility, and suspicion that would be aroused by partisan defections or backroom deals on a decision of such magnitude could be extremely damaging to the internal workings of the Congress. Nor should we forget the desirability of an independent executive. There is a highly persuasive case for insulating the Presidency from the process of political negotiation in Congress.

The contingency election takes on the guise of a dilemma: a straight partisan vote would make it impossible for the congressional minority party's candidate to win; coalition-building through partisan defections would result in bitterness and suspicions of corrupt deals that might damage the Congress as well as the Presidency. The argument for the joint-session plan rests on the assumption that a President chosen by a joint session would be more rep-

resentative of the popular will than one chosen by the
House voting by states. This assumption is not warranted,
given the demonstrable partisan incongruence between the
Congress and the Presidency; the majority party in Congress is not always the party of the President. Because the
joint-session plan does not destroy the potential bias against
the congressional minority party's candidate, its implementation would have theoretical rather than practical value.
It is not at all clear that the suggested system would be a
substantive improvement. In fact, neither the existing contingency procedure nor the joint-session plan is completely
satisfactory.

Perhaps the simplest reform would be to convert the
requirement for victory from a majority of the electoral
votes to a simple plurality of electoral votes. This plan
would eliminate the problem of intrigue and political bargaining in the Congress and would make the general election the only election. There has been little support for this
proposal, because it is feared it could produce a President
with an insufficient mandate.

It is patent that some procedure is necessary in order to
avoid a constitutional crisis. A single election is preferable
because uncertainty and delayed decisions can foster discord and discredit our institutions. A swift, sharp decision
will be quickly accepted and will insure continuity of
government. In evaluating any contingency-election procedure, the first question should be, How often would a contingency election be necessary? The probability of a contingency election has a direct bearing on its most desirable
form, for if the results of a general election are frequently

inconclusive, we must seriously consider bringing the people into the contingency process. If the general election does not produce a winner much of the time, a contingency election that is removed from the people will not satisfy democratic criteria. If, however, the general election rarely fails to select a President or does so only under unusual circumstances, we must consider the most prudent and expeditious method of resolving a deadlock.

A praiseworthy fact about the present general-election system is that it has never failed. Since the passage of the Twelfth Amendment the nation has had only one contingency election, in 1824, but the present system, with the unit rule, did not evolve until 1832. In 1824 the country was in a period of one-party dominance, with no national conventions to control access to candidacy, and the unit rule had not been universally adopted. The unit rule and the national conventions that have evolved to become essential features of the electoral process are largely responsible for the success of the general election. As I have argued in the previous chapter, the present system inflates the plurality winner's percentage of the electoral vote and, therefore, largely precludes the possibility of a contingency election.

In 1824 only half of the states selected their electors under the unit rule. By 1832 all but two had adopted the unit rule; in that year the parties first turned to the national-convention system. The unit rule and the national convention system interact and reinforce each other to produce a plurality system and a single election. Through the convention system the parties have established firm control over potential candidates and have been able to maintain that control because the unit system converts statewide pluralities into total statewide victories and as a rule converts popular pluralities into electoral majorities. Since the general election is going to be the only election, a man who goes against his party convention's choice will split the party and destroy its chance of victory. He will, in the process, earn the enmity of powerful party figures who, if they can, will punish him in the future. On the other hand, if he goes along with his party's choice he will, no doubt, share in the spoils of victory. The unit rule thus hands the parties both the carrot and the stick with which to control intractable faction leaders. The election of 1912, when the Republicans split, is a classic example of what happens when a party cannot control access to candidacy. A divided party creates a landslide for its opposition. Wilson won only 42 percent of the popular vote, but this gave him 82 percent of the electoral vote—a distortion of 40 percent.

As long as a majority of the electoral votes is required for victory the possibility of a contingency election persists, but as long as the unit rule continues in effect the possibility of a House election is exceedingly remote. Critics suggest that the danger of deadlock is especially acute when the popular contest is close or when a strong third-party movement develops. As Tables 3 and 4 indicate, the possibility that a deadlock will result from a close popular election is overrated. In 1880, when only 0.1 percent of the popular vote separated the two major candidates, Garfield won with an electoral majority of 58 percent. As for the danger of deadlocks resulting from third-party movements, the historical evidence should hearten the alarmists. The republic has had eleven elections since 1824 in which a third or fourth candidate won more than 1 percent of the electoral votes. In every case the electoral system, through the unit rule, gave the plurality candidate a decisive victory, as Table 5 indicates.

Table 5. Winner's percentage of the electoral vote in years when more than two candidates won electoral votes

Year	Winner's % of electoral vote	% disparity between winner's electoral and popular vote
1832	76.5	22.0
1836	57.8	6.7
1856	58.7	13.1
1860	59.4	19.7
1872	81.9	26.3
1892	62.3	16.3
1912	81.9	40.1
1924	71.7	17.7
1948	57.0	7.5
1960	56.4	6.7
1968	55.9	12.5

Although the historical evidence indicates that the potential for failure in the general election is greatly exaggerated, fears that the general election will fail have been largely responsible for swelling the ranks of critics. The general election failed in 1824 because there were five serious candidates, and the potential for failure is directly related to multicandidacies. Because of the unit rule, however, a third-party candidate cannot provoke a House election if his popular strength is spread throughout the nation, for he will probably fail to win any electoral votes. On the other hand, a third party candidate who has a sectional base can win electoral votes. This built-in discrimination against national third parties is strikingly illustrated by the election of 1948, when Henry Wallace, Progressive, and Strom Thurmond, States' Rights, polled 2.38 and 2.40 percent respectively, of the popular vote. Yet Wallace did not win a single electoral vote, and Thurmond won thirty-nine. A national third party can hold the balance of power and can throw the victory one way or another, but it cannot throw the election to the House unless it has sufficient sectional strength to win electoral votes.

While it is possible that a sectional third party could win enough votes to deprive either major candidate of a majority, this is far more difficult than it would appear, as those who have tried it can testify. To create a deadlock a third party must draw votes away from both major parties. If it takes too much from one, it will create a landslide for the other. The election of 1836 demonstrates the difficulty of throwing an election to the House. Though there were four candidates, three were Whigs. The Democratic candidate, Van Buren, had far less appeal than his mentor Jackson yet won easily, with 57.8 percent of the electoral vote. In 1836 the Whigs did not hold a national convention. Their strategy was to defeat Van Buren by running a series of favorite sons, thus preventing an electoral majority and throwing the election into the House. The Tennessee and Alabama legislatures nominated Senator Hugh L. White for the Southern Whigs; the Massachusetts legislature nominated Daniel Webster for the New England Whigs; and a Pennsylvania state convention nominated William Harrison, who was popular in the Western states. The idea of exploiting local feelings by running strong sectional candidates was clever but was not enough to overcome a united Democratic party. Multiple candidacies alone appear unlikely to create an electoral deadlock, especially when the political controversy is framed in terms of the ins versus the outs, and the ins possess a formidable party machinery and the outs are disunited. Svend Petersen suggests that the shift of 14,061 votes in New York would have created a deadlock, but these would have constituted 4.6 percent of the total statewide vote.[4] A shift of this magnitude would hardly be limited to one state.

In 1848 there arose a third party that managed to amass a significant portion of the popular vote. The Free Soil party candidate, Van Buren, won 10.13 percent of the national vote. The new party was in part a response to the discontented, antislavery, antisouthern factions in both major parties. Lewis Cass, the Democratic candidate, opposed the Wilmot Proviso forbidding slavery in any territory obtained from Mexico and favored squatter sovereignty. The Whig candidate, Zachary Taylor, was a Louisiana slaveholder. The Free Soil party hoped to draw potential defectors from the other two parties. It did attract significant numbers of Democrats, particularly in New York. But even the burning question of slavery did not bring many dissident Whigs into the camp of their old enemy Van Buren. A third party is often hard-pressed to find a

4. *A Statistical History of the American Presidential Elections* (New York, 1968), p. 22.

prominent national figure who is acceptable to dissidents in both major parties. If, as in 1848, the third-party candidate is unacceptable to dissidents in one of the major parties, they will return to their traditional party or they will not vote at all. Unless a thirty-party candidate can wring votes from both parties, an election will not be thrown into the House but will be won by the party which has the tighter hold on its own potential defectors. In the election of 1848, the Free Soil movement was more a reflection of a division in the Democratic party than of a division in both major parties. Therefore the Whigs won.

The Dixiecrat revolt in 1948, designed to prove that the national Democratic party needed southern electoral votes, was, according to V. O. Key, more a fantasy than a real threat to the victory of one of the two major parties.[5] In 1968, George Wallace and his American Independence party tried to convert the fantasy into a reality. He ran a national campaign; with a little help from the Supreme Court, his name was entered on the ballot in all fifty states. He polled 13.5 percent of the popular vote. He polled under 3 percent in only two states, over 5 percent in forty-two states, and over 10 percent in twenty-three states. Clearly, Wallace has some national appeal. His success in northern industrial states has deeply shaken state and local politicians. (He won 8 percent of the vote in Pennsylvania, 8.5 in Illinois, 9 in New Jersey, 10 in Michigan, 11 in Indiana, and 11.8 in Ohio.) What he did accomplish was to change the balance of power in a number of states. One election analyst, Kevin Phillips, claims that the Wallace

5. *Southern Politics* (New York, 1969), p. 6.

vote hurt Nixon more than Humphrey, because although much of the Wallace vote, even in the North, was nominally Democratic, it was wrung from that conservative, disaffected group of Democrats who might otherwise have voted for Nixon.[6] Nixon's own advisers saw the Wallace candidacy as dividing the antiadministration vote, and they devised a campaign strategy designed to protect Nixon's right flank.[7] On the other hand, the Ripon Society, a Republican research and policy organization, in its report and analysis of the 1968 election, concludes that "the gains and losses occasioned by Wallace canceled each other out." It found that Wallace hurt Nixon in the South, particularly in Texas, where the majority of Wallace's 600,000 votes would probably have gone to Nixon in a two-way race. In Texas, Humphrey's winning margin was only 39,000 votes. According to this analysis, Nixon's losses in the South were balanced by Humphrey's losses in Alaska, Delaware, Illinois, Missouri, New Jersey, and Ohio.[8]

Whether Wallace's deadlock strategy failed because his candidacy drew equally on the strength of both parties or because he could not capture enough of the antiadministration, incipient Republican vote, its threat was sufficient to rouse both major candidates. Both Nixon and Humphrey stressed the fact that Wallace could only be a spoiler; he could not win the Presidency, and a vote for him would be

6. *The Emerging Republican Majority* (New Rochelle, N.Y., 1969), p. 34.

7. Ripon Society, *The Lessons of Victory* (New York, 1969), p. 6.

8. *Ibid.*, p. 213.

a vote wasted.[9] Wallace himself admitted that he would probably have little chance in the House and that his plan was to decide the election in the electoral college. He collected affidavits from all his electors which pledged them to vote for him or for the man of his choice in the college.[10]

The wasted-vote argument is particularly effective. It is one thing to tell a pollster you favor the third runner; it is another to vote for him on election day, particularly when you don't have a second chance to vote. If the contest appears close, voters will often resist the temptation to cast a protest vote, in order to insure the victory of the man they would prefer in a two-way race or, perhaps more accurately, to insure the defeat of the candidate they oppose. Furthermore, the major candidates are not likely to sit idly and allow a third candidate to walk off with some of their followers. Therefore, both Nixon and Humphrey adapted their campaign strategies to the Wallace threat and raised issues designed to bring voters back to their traditional folds or to counteract the Wallace appeal.

Another reason for the furor over the Wallace candidacy was that many believed his American Independence party was rightist. Historically, the country's strong third parties have generally been leftist–Socialists, Populists, Progressives. And they have been tolerated and even praised by political analysts as parties of reform, sources of new ideas, experimenters with new issues.[11] Clearly the popular

9. *Ibid.*, p. 103.
10. *Ibid.*, p. 111.
11. William Hesseltine, *Third Party Movements in the United States* (New York, 1962).

appeal of the Wallace candidacy did, in 1968, move both parties somewhat to the right.

In 1968, the Wallace candidacy, as has been the case with all strong third-party movements, brought to light the nature of popular discontent; it signaled to the other parties the degree and the distribution of disaffection. Because our major parties are generally conceded to be power-oriented, and because 13 percent of the vote is a prize worth some effort, one might have prophesied that the defeated party, the Democrats, would make strenuous efforts to capture this vote in the next election. However, although reformers have long been tolerant of, or indulgent toward, third parties of the left, third parties of the right arouse fear and indignation. While leaders of the "party of change" have been quick to deem a strong showing by a leftist party a "new political reality," they are not as easily convinced by a strong showing on the right. This phenomenon may in part explain why Democratic party leaders were reluctant to oppose the McGovern Commission's delegate-selection reform (which led to such an unrepresentative national convention) and their apparent blindness to the significant defections of traditional Democrats to Wallace and Nixon in 1968.

In 1972 the Democrats did not hearken to the signal sent up in 1968 or to the impressive Wallace primary victories in 1972. It seems clear that the election was lost at the nominating convention. In selecting a candidate who was perceived by part of the electorate as a radical or a man of the far left, the Democrats suffered their worst presidential defeat. With an estimated three-fourths of the Wallace vote going to Nixon in 1972, the Democratic party lost the blue-collar vote, the Catholic vote, and the entire South for the first time since Reconstruction (Arkansas went Republican for the first time in one hundred years). In light of the results in 1972, Kevin Phillips' analysis of the 1968 election and his prediction in 1969 that the Democratic party would pay a heavy price for ignoring the signals of 1968 and locking itself to the left appear remarkably foresighted. Within eight years the nation has been treated to an object lesson in politics. Two of the greatest landslides in our history occurred in close proximity—in 1964 and 1972—and in both cases the defeated candidate was perceived by the electorate as an extremist. In American presidential politics, the center will hold; moderation is the watchword at the gates of presidential victory.

Whatever problems the Wallace phenomenon may have brought to light, we may take comfort in the fact that it illustrated anew the impracticality of a third-party strategy whose object is to deadlock an election. In 1968, Wallace won 4,100,000 votes outside the South and not a single electoral vote. His popular percentage of 13.5 was converted into an electoral percentage of 8. He won only 6 more electoral votes than Thurmond won in 1948. To bring off a deadlock strategy a third candidate must walk a very narrow path. First he must have a strong regional base where he can win electoral votes. Then he must wage a national campaign for popular votes that produces a fairly even electoral vote division between the two major candidates in order to prevent the stronger candidate from getting an electoral majority. If the major parties are evenly matched in potential electoral votes, he must draw equally on the strength of both. If they are not, he must draw more from the stronger. But during the course of the campaign the relative positions of the two major candidates continuously fluctuate. Moreover, the major candidates can use the wasted-vote argument, and they can and will style their campaigns to give positive signals to potential protest voters. The third-party candidate is in the situation of a parachutist attempting to land on a marker with the winds strong and variable.

The much maligned electoral system effectively provides us with a single election. The fears of the critics on this score are largely exaggerated. Dwelling on the horrible consequences of a deadlock has blinded them to the improbability of its occurrence. The electoral college minimizes third-party strength. For all his effort and expense, Wallace did not improve significantly on Thurmond's electoral-vote percentage in 1948. He did, however, greatly surpass Thurmond's popular percentage. This fact has a great bearing on our evaluation of the direct election and its contingency provision. The direct-election plan provides for a national runoff if no candidate attains a 40 percent plurality of the popular vote. In a direct election a third-party candidate could more easily force a runoff, because only the popular votes would be counted. It is much easier for a third-party candidate to win a significant percentage of the popular vote than of the electoral vote.

Direct election, in itself, would open the door to multiple candidacies. The unit rule, which has worked to reinforce the conventions' control over candidates, would be abolished, and candidates rejected by the conventions could take their case to the people freed of the bonds of winning statewide pluralities. Nor would it be necessary for a candidate to initiate a nationwide campaign. He could concentrate his appeals in such regions as the populous eastern megalopolis. Moreover, there are many reasons why a candidate will enter the lists. A good chance of winning is but one. Dissatisfied factions may, as the Dixiecrats did in 1948, enter a candidate to prove to their national party that it needs their votes. Others may wish to give their cause national exposure or to test the depth of popular sentiment on a current issue. But the seeds of too many candidacies planted in the same electoral plot will prevent full maturation, with no one blooming into a majority victor. The reformers have no wish to see the two party-system stifled in an election crowded with candidates. Therefore they have included in their amendment a mechanism which they believe will rid the electoral process of unwanted multiple candidacies. This mechanism is the 40-percent-plurality rule.

Ironically, a vocal minority in the House found this proposal undemocratic. Congressman John Dowdy, the most persistent critic of the 40-percent rule, saw it as a deliberate distortion of the one man, one vote principle.

The proponents of direct election claim they want to effectuate the "one man, one vote" slogan. But they immediately provide that a President shall be elected by 40 percent of the voters, which effectively belies the "one man, one vote" claim. The real meaning of the 40 percent provision is "one man, 1½ votes." Under this "one man, 1½ votes" provision, as I have mentioned earlier, it would mean that a man could be elected President who was bitterly opposed by three out of five voters. If this is "one man, one vote," I do not understand the English language.[12]

The gravest objection to the proposed plurality requirement is that it would result in frequent runoffs. The 40-percent rule was designed to cure the defects in our present system, but this cure would prove to be worse than the disease.

The American Bar Association commission's rationale for choosing the 40-percent figure was explained by John D. Feerick, who testified:

The commission felt that the required vote should be high enough to furnish a sufficient mandate for the Presidency and, at the same time, be low enough so that one election would decide the contest. . . . In deciding upon a 40 percent requirement, the commission was also influenced by the view that too low a figure might have the effect of weakening our two party structure, since the chances of a minority candidate becoming President would be increased. On the other hand, the commission felt that a figure much higher than 40 percent might have the same effect, since a minority party would be better able to determine the outcome of an election or cause the election to be resolved under the contingency election procedure.[13]

The commission concluded that a 40-percent requirement

12. *Congressional Record*, Vol. 115, Pt. 19, 91st Cong., 1st sess. (1969), p. 25134.

13. U.S., Senate, Committee on the Judiciary, Subcommittee on Constitutional Amendments, *Hearings, Election of the President*, 89th Cong., 2d sess., and 90th Cong., 1st sess., 1968, p. 320 (cited hereafter as 1968 Senate *Hearings*).

would make a runoff remote; yet it acknowledges that either a higher or a lower percentage might encourage multiple candidates. The faith these men have in the 40-percent figure is remarkable. One may wonder if there is something magical about 40 percent. The foundation of their case is, however, not magic but history.

The commission was influenced by the fact that 14 Presidents received less than 50 percent of the popular vote—11 between 45 and 50 percent; one [as of 1974, 2] between 40 and 45 percent; one (Lincoln) 39 percent, but his name did not appear on the ballot in 10 States; and one (J. Q. Adams) 30 percent (but in that election Jackson received 43 percent of the popular vote, although in six of the 24 States the electors were not chosen by the people).[14]

What past election history indicates is that the present system is unlikely to produce a deadlock—it never has. Past election history cannot support the argument that the 40-percent rule makes runoffs remote, because when we change the rules, we change the game. Under the rules of the proposed amendment, campaign strategy and candidate and issue selection could and would be changed.

Despite the fact that both the chairman of the Judiciary Committee and its ranking member endorsed the ABA's historical case, the plan aroused great concern, particularly about the Lincoln election. Congressman David Dennis asked in the House hearings whether Lincoln would have been elected if the 40 percent runoff rule had been in force. We must remember that any change in the rules would have worked changes in the general election itself. How-

14. *Ibid.*

ever, the answer to Congressman Dennis' question would appear to be No.

There were four candidates in 1860: Lincoln, Stephen Douglas, John Breckinridge, and John Bell. It was not a four-way contest nationally but, rather, Lincoln against Douglas in the North, and Bell against Breckinridge in the South. In a runoff, assuming, as the ABA apparently does, that a change in the rules would not have changed the result of the general election, the contestants would have been Lincoln and Douglas. None of Breckinridge's followers would have gone over to Lincoln; if they voted at all, it would have been for Douglas, as by far the lesser evil. And it seems safe to believe that little of Bell's support would have gone to Lincoln. Except for Massachusetts, Bell had negligible support in the North. His real strength lay in the South and the Border States, where again Douglas would probably have been preferred. Of the four candidates, Bell and Douglas were considered the moderates; given a second chance, the moderates may well have fused.

On the floor of the House in 1969 there was considerable division among the members on the 40-percent figure. Congressman Byron Rogers offered a substitute amendment requiring a 45-percent plurality, and Congressman Joe Waggonner offered one requiring 50 percent. Their proposals were prompted by fears that a plurality of 40 percent did not constitute a proper mandate and was not in keeping with the principle of majority rule. Both amendments were rejected on the grounds that they would increase the likelihood of runoffs and inflate the chances of splinter parties. Other congressmen feared that the 40-percent figure was too high, and Congressman Hamilton Fish offered a substitute of 35 percent, in order to prevent runoffs. His amendment, too, was defeated, on the grounds that a plurality of 35 percent constituted an insufficient mandate.

A runoff is clearly undesirable; aside from the expense to the parties and to the states, the electorate wearies of elections. Experience in gubernatorial runoffs shows that there has often been a drop in the rate of turnout between the first primary and the runoff. V. O. Key cites a study of thirty-eight such runoffs between 1919 and 1948 and the turnout declined in thirty.[15]

A runoff extends the electorate's uncertainty, and uncertainty fosters political intrigue and increases the likelihood of violence, as the election of 1876 demonstrates. A runoff extends candidate uncertainty and could sharply shorten the time available for the orderly transition of power. The President-elect needs sufficient time to make his appointments, to form his cabinet, to be briefed on all aspects of the national situation. This problem might be resolved by holding the general election earlier to allow time for a runoff. However, extension of the period between the general election and the inauguration is undesirable, since it would delay the implementation of the popular will. This interval has many of the characteristics of an interregnum, especially from the perspective of foreign nations. Indeed, we amended the Constitution in order to reduce this period.

A further problem raised by the 40-percent plan is that a national recount to determine if in fact any candidate re-

15. *Southern Politics*, p. 419.

ceived 40 percent of the vote might well be necessary. Charges of fraud or simple errors in tabulation might result in contests all over the nation. And all the while the results would be in doubt. The leading candidate would not know if he was the President-elect or merely the front runner in the initial contest. Both he and the runner-up would have to keep open channels to potential rebels, to probe for soft spots in their opponents' followings. Potential defectors might approach the front runners with offers of support. The political wheeling and dealing would continue. The top candidates would have to prepare for the possibility of a new election, and they might continue to campaign.

Frequent runoffs would weaken or alter our two-party system, on whose benefits there is almost universal agreement. Some proponents of the direct-election plan deny that their reform would injure the two-party system in any substantive way because they believe the electoral college is an independent variable, that the form of the electoral process has little or no effect on the character of the party system. This is as great an error in judgment as its opposite, the belief that structural or institutional factors are the sole cause of a party system. The fact is that we do not know with any certainty what the basic supports or causes are. Many political scientists credit the single-member-district, plurality-election system as a primary force behind the two-party system. Few, if any, are so rash as to say it is the only or the sufficient cause.

Several direct-election proponents apparently concede that these institutional factors may support congressional two-partyism, but they deny any similar force to the presidential-electoral process, though it demonstrably works in the same way. It is in practice a plurality system which not only magnifies the plurality winner's margin of victory over the runner-up but also gives the runner-up the monopoly of opposition. In the face of this, it is rash to suggest that "any intelligent appraisal of the nature and consequences of runoff elections, then, must be based on the character of the electorate, and of the political parties *as we now know them*."[16] To say this is to forget that when we change the rules, we change the game; and when we change the game, we may be changing the size, strength, talent, and character of those who can play the game and play it well.

Nonetheless, Harvey Zeidenstein argues that the existence and viability of the two-party system cannot be attributed to the electoral-college system, and therefore its abandonment would have no dysfunctional or undesirable effects on the two-party system.[17] His argument is not convincing because he does not consider the significance of a party's nominating function or the fact that the adoption of the unit rule has made the electoral system one of single-member districts with statewide pluralities. These two factors interrelate and reinforce each other. Whether either was the definitive "cause" of the two-party system may be a fruitless inquiry. What is very apparent throughout our history is that they are mutually advantageous and supportive. Since the adoption of the unit rule we have had no

16. Harvey Zeidenstein, *Direct Election of the President* (Lexington, Mass., 1973), p. 73; my italics.
17. *Ibid.*, pp. 56–59.

contingency elections, nor are we likely to have one. The fact that this avenue, this second chance, is closed means that many potential factional candidates have little to gain and a great deal to lose by refusing to accept their party's nomination as a definitive point of no return. Zeidenstein argues that under a direct-election plan factional candidates would be deterred by their awareness that their effort might be dysfunctional and throw the election to the party or candidate they would find least acceptable.[18] But even under the admittedly severe disadvantages of the unit rule, we have had several factional candidates who refused to accept their party's nomination procedures as final. If they have done so under the unit rule, which makes a second election so unlikely, what would they do under the direct-election, 40-percent runoff rule?

The proponents of the direct-election plan base their case on the abstract principles of populistic democracy. Yet, as Max S. Power points out in his analysis of the requirements of popular sovereignty and majority rule, unless there are only two alternatives the populistic requirements may not be met.[19] He states that "direct election provides no workable means for selecting a president from among more than two candidates,"[20] and he accuses the direct-election proponents of assuming "two party competition without ask-

18. *Ibid.*

19. "Logic and Legitimacy: On Understanding the Electoral College Controversy," in *Perspectives on Presidential Selection*, ed. Donald R. Matthews (Washington, 1973), p. 221.

20. *Ibid.*, p. 205.

ing how their proposals are related to it," thus ignoring "the logical problems of multi-candidate contests."[21]

Many political analysts focus on the importance of the parties' nomination function and have suggested that control over nominations may be a necessary condition of our moderate two-party system. The significance of nomination arises from the parties' ability to sift and select a limited number of credible candidates, thereby structuring the choice for the people. The task of nominating the President is what brings together and temporarily binds our "loose leagues of state and local parties."[22] The winning of the Presidency is the focal point of our national parties and perhaps their reason for being. Their strength depends on their control over the access to candidacy. V. O. Key gives this rule of thumb: "Those who control the party organization often control access to the general election ballot and hence the access to public office."[23] E. E. Schattschneider goes so far as to say, "If a party cannot make nominations it ceases to be a party." But he goes even further and makes a distinction between nominations and real nominations; it is the latter which are the distinguishing marks of modern political parties.

Whether or not a nomination is a real nomination depends on whether or not it is binding, whether it effectively commits the whole party to support it. If it is binding, if all other

21. *Ibid.*, p. 232.
22. E. E. Schattschneider, *Party Government* (New York, 1967), p. 83.
23. *Southern Politics*, p. 387.

candidates within the party (for the office in question) are denied party support, and if the party is able to concentrate its strength behind the designated candidate, a nomination has been made *regardless of the process by which it is made.*[24]

Under a direct election, the national parties would continue to make nominations, but whether these nominations would be binding or, in Schattschneider's terminology, real nominations, is another question.

Dissatisfied party factions look for loopholes in any nomination process, and the proposed reform, with its 40-percent runoff rule, would give them a second chance. The present system's solution to incipient multifactionalism and to third parties, whether national or sectional, is the unit rule. It reinforces the conventions' control over access to candidacy. It converted Wallace's 13.5 percent of the popular vote into 8 percent of the electoral vote. The critics' assertion that it favors sectional third parties is true only in a limited sense. It does give a sectional third party electoral votes under the winner-take-all rule. But—and this is the point the critics appear to forget—a truly sectional party will not win an election.

Presidents can be elected only by a combination of sections, by parties that cross sectional lines. . . . Sooner or later exclusively sectional parties are likely to lose even their sectional support in favor of a major party which has a real chance of winning the supreme prize. . . . The two party system is firmly established because the second major party is able to

24. *Party Government*, p. 64.

defend itself against purely sectional parties as well as against all other varieties of minor parties.[25]

Under the unit rule, between 1840 and 1968, third and fourth candidates won only 261 electoral votes out of 14,-462. While the distortion between the popular vote and the electoral vote favors the winner over the runner-up, that same distortion process almost completely excludes third and fourth candidates from the electoral college.

There are, to be sure, noninstitutional supports for two-partyism, among them "the character of social conflict and consensus in the nation."[26] The tradition of consensus politics and the nonideological cast of the voters contribute to stability and two-partyism. But the raw materals for deep divisions are present in any nation. By fostering accommodation, by giving something to every major interest group but fully satisfying none at the expense of another, the parties may inhibit the development of latent ideological divisions.

Political scientists have yet to resolve the thorny question of whether it is the social and political elements or the institutional electoral rules that determine the nature of the party system. This question may never be resolved, and the viability of the two-party system may remain somewhat of a mystery. Yet the historical evidence of the electoral-college discrimination against third and fourth candidates cannot be denied. It may be that American two-partyism is

25. *Ibid.*, pp. 83–84.
26. Allan P. Sindler, *Political Parties in the United States* (New York, 1966), p. 57.

supported by both institutional and noninstitutional factors. If we dare to kick away one pillar, will the burden be too much for the other to bear? The proponents of the direct election recognize the problem and believe that the 40-percent-plurality runoff rule will be an institutional support of the two-party system.

They argue that it would be very difficult for a splinter party to poll the 20 percent or more of the vote necessary to produce a runoff. This argument is not convincing. Even under the unit rule, splinter candidates have done well in the popular vote. In 1856, Millard Fillmore received 21 percent of the popular vote; in 1860, the third- and fourth-ranking candidates' combined total was 30.8 percent; in 1912, William Howard Taft, the third runner in the popular contest, received 23 percent; in 1924, Robert La Follette attained 16.6 percent. These candidates all ran well, despite the fact that the major parties could use the wasted-vote argument against them.

If candidates could run so well in spite of the unit rule, they surely could do even better if released from its bonds. In 1968, George Wallace alone obtained nearly 14 percent of the popular vote, and if the proposed amendment had been in effect, Eugene McCarthy might not have been able or willing to resist the pressures that would have developed for his entry, which would probably have forced a runoff in 1968 under the 40-percent rule. The very entrance of a third candidate would in itself provide the incentive for a fourth and even a fifth entry. The more candidates, the greater their cumulative power to force a runoff. In a scenario describing the 1968 election as though it had been held under the rules of the proposed amendment, Nelson Rockefeller follows hard on McCarthy's heels, and Ronald Reagan decides he will not be left waiting at the gate. The snowball sets off an avalanche, with the result that "at the end of October the *New York Times* has to publish a twenty-four page supplement to tell the voters who is who —and what."[27]

The problem is not merely that such an avalanche would be destructive of the two-party system, but also that the more moderate candidate, the second choice of a majority, might be excluded from the runoff. To say, as some critics have, that a runoff solves this kind of dissensus is to ignore the possibility of a runoff between extremist candidates. Zeidenstein suggests that this could occur "only if the over whelming majority of the voters were, themselves, polarized into two extreme groups."[28] But it could also occur if the moderates split in a multicandidate race. In a general election with six to ten candidates, the split in the moderate votes might result in a runoff between the more extreme candidates. This kind of split is frequently characteristic of preconvention politics and primary systems. Indeed, many analysts suggested that it was a factor in the 1972 Democratic primaries. The direct-election advocates suggest that prenomination multifactionalism is distinguishable from that of a general election because in the latter unity is insured by the desirability of defeating the opposite party. However, the runoff might turn the general election into a national primary. The pressures for unity are great when

27. *Time*, 95 (May 4, 1970), 26.
28. *Direct Election*, p. 72.

the general election is the final election, not when it may be the first stage in the selection process.

Under the unit rule multiple candidacies alone will not cause the general election to fail, because only candidates who can win statewide pluralities can win electoral votes. In the thirty-three elections since 1840, we have had thirty-one when more than two candidates won popular votes, and in only nine of these elections did a third candidate win electoral votes. In no case did these candidates force a contingency election, despite the fact that in twenty-six of these elections there were five or more candidates. Millard Fillmore may have won 21 percent of the popular vote, but he won only 2 percent of the electoral vote. William H. Taft won 23 percent of the popular vote, but he won only 1.5 percent of the electoral vote. If only the popular votes were counted a third candidate could more readily force a runoff than when the popular votes are converted into electoral votes.

The proponents of the direct-election plan focus on the possibility of third-party movements triggering a runoff. James Kirby, who argues that it would be extremely difficult for a third party to get 20 percent of the popular vote, believes that third parties may be valuable prods to the major parties. He suggests that if a third party could win such a percentage, "then, perhaps, this may be one of those third parties which is going to replace one of the major parties."[29] True third parties, however, would only be a contributing danger. The real danger lies not so much in the proliferation of parties as in the fragmentation of the

29. Statement of James Kirby, 1968 Senate *Hearings*, p. 332.

major parties. Common sense suggests that malcontents will not abide by the verdict of the party conventions if they are given the opportunity for an appeal. And discontented factions often take an extreme position on some issue which the main body of the party finds inexpedient. The prospect of winning policy concessions for support in a runoff may lead single-issue or doctrinaire groups to enter a candidate.

Voter psychology contributes to the problem. Donald Stokes argues:

If you put in the runoff, you turn that first election from something that is going to dispose of the office to something that might just be a preliminary to the real election, then it seems to me that you do run the risk of encouraging people to get into that first election who would not otherwise be credible candidates. You also encourage the voters to support candidates that they otherwise would not think about.[30]

Most presidential contests have been cast in the form of the ins versus the outs. But if the conventions lose control over the nominating process, the monopoly of opposition could be broken. The voters might be given two or three alternatives to the ins, and with the opposition divided, the ins could become entrenched. The 1968 election is interesting in this regard. Theodore H. White called it a negative landslide in which "Americans turned against the whole set of Democratic policy and leadership of the previous four years—but could not make up their minds in which new direction they would move."[31] His argument, an argument that Kevin Phillips develops and extends in his book, *The*

30. Statement of Donald Stokes, *ibid.*, p. 571.
31. *The Making of the President, 1968* (New York, 1969), p. 397.

Emerging Republican Majority, is that the negative land-slide was concealed by Nixon's slim margin of victory. The outs were divided; the combined Nixon and Wallace vote was 56.9 percent, but Nixon's margin over Humphrey was only 0.7 percent. This division of the outs very nearly returned the ins despite the negative landslide.

In the 1968 campaign both Nixon and Humphrey used the classic wasted-vote argument to turn voters away from Wallace. But the possibility of a runoff would change the voter's reply. A voter who felt strongly might accept the risk of casting a wasted vote in order to cast a protest vote, particularly if he believed he had a fair chance to vote again. In such circumstances people would be inclined to vote for a more extreme candidate than they ordinarily would.

Candidate psychology would also enter in. Self-nominated or factional leaders might focus on the current campaign and their own chances. Thus they could be willing to take more extreme positions than the party as a whole, which must be concerned about future contests. V. O. Key has suggested that "individualistic or disorganized politics places a high premium on demagogic qualities of personality that attract voter attention," whereas "party machinery, in the advancement of leaders, is apt to reject those with rough edges and angular qualities out of preference for more conformist personalities."[32] Thus one of the most frightening prospects is that the runoff could institute a cycle of inferior candidates.

32. *Southern Politics*, p. 304.

Key's extensive study of southern state politics led him to suggest that "it may well be that multi-factional states are multi-factional because of the existence of the runoff."[33] While Key stated this as a theory and not as an ironclad rule, it may give us pause. Although his empirical findings were mixed, he concluded that "they give some support to the hypothesis that the runoff encourages a multiplicity of factions."[34] An explanation is that the possibility of a runoff undercuts the incentive for coalition-building prior to the first election. Congressman William Clay may have touched on the vital point when he argued that "it is not an instinctive desire for unity—but a fear of losing all impact outside the two parties—which keeps this delicate machine together and which promotes compromise, co-operation and understanding of the interests and views which must be reflected in the total party."[35]

The southern state-office runoffs occurred under state-wide majority requirements. Under the proposed presidential system, the requirement would be 40 percent. Lowering the requirement might not, however, be sufficient to avoid party fragmentation. Aspiration to the office of President is not lightly abandoned, and pressures from followers emotionally attached to some particular policy may be formidable. It is much easier to build a following by taking an extreme position against something than to build one by proposing a positive course of corrective action.

33. *Ibid.*, p. 417.
34. *Ibid.*, p. 421.
35. *Congressional Record*, Vol. 115, Pt. 19, 91st Cong., 1st sess. (1969), p. 25391.

Thus the second-chance psychology that could infect both candidates and voters might not be counteracted by a reduced percentage requirement. There is nothing magical about the 40-percent figure; it was a compromise choice. In the final analysis, it is not so much the percentage required as the fact that there is a percentage requirement that creates the danger.

A simple plurality requirement would be the solution in the abstract; it would institute a single election. But a simple plurality requirement appears too radical a notion to many congressmen and would very likely defeat the reform. Visions of a 20-percent President haunt our congressmen; the belief abounds, as expressed by Senator Bayh, that "there is a floor below which one cannot go if a serious lack of confidence on the part of the public is to be avoided."[36]

Instead of preventing multifactionalism, instead of securing party convention control over access to candidacy, the 40-percent runoff rule would do the opposite. With the entry of multiple candidates the general election could be transformed into a national primary. Although the national-convention system has many faults and improvements in its operation may be desirable, it has many advantages over a national primary. When the selection process is controlled by professional party leaders whose object is power, the candidates are more likely to be men with a broad appeal. The convention system promotes party unity, compromise, and conciliation. It tempers and welds together the discordant elements within the party. Under a national-primary system there would be a risk of fostering long-lasting di-

36. 1968 Senate *Hearings*, p. 599.

visions within a party when rivalry among the party leaders was intensified and nationally publicized. And in a national primary, there would be no assurance that the most generally preferred candidate would be chosen. In a three-way race the man in the middle could come in last.

Aside from the possibility that the general election might be transformed into a national primary by the entry of multiple candidates, there is the additional problem of the legal institution of a national primary. The language of the proposed amendment, giving Congress reserve power to make or alter regulations providing for entitlement to inclusion on the ballot, could be construed to permit Congress to require a national primary. Several congressmen raised the question on the House floor in an attempt to clarify the intention of the House. Many who supported the amendment did not wish to abolish the national-convention system. The legislative history is not clear, however. Congressman McCulloch, the ranking member of the Judiciary Committee, noted that there had been no discussion of the matter in committee and, therefore, no decision on congressional power to institute a national primary.[37]

If the amendment were passed, there would be pressure to construe its language broadly and require a national primary, since there are some who believe that a "direct popular election is worse than meaningless where there is no direct popular nomination."[38] An editorial in the *Southern*

37. *Congressional Record*, Vol. 115, Pt. 19, 91st Cong., 1st sess. (1969), p. 25136.
38. "The Presidential Nomination: Equal Protection at the Grass Roots," *Southern California Law Review* 42 (Fall 1968), 169.

California Law Review argued that the equal-protection clause, as interpreted by the Baker line of cases, is violated when the party members do not have equally weighted votes in the nominating process.

Nomination and election are but component parts of a single process, and interference with participation at one stage should be as constitutionally impermissible as interference with participation at the other. In allowing the "party" to exercise full control over nomination, a court is allowing a small number of individuals to substitute their judgment for that of the electorate which, in effect, is a form of vote-dilution.[39]

There appears to be no limit to which some analysts will extend the Baker line of cases. They will have equally weighted votes in the nominating process even if the most widely preferred candidate, everyone's second choice, is eliminated in the primary. They fail to realize that a national primary with equally weighted votes is less likely to produce the moderate candidates favored by the majority than the national conventions dominated by party professionals. The advantages of the national party conventions are too great to be abandoned in the search for equally weighted votes.

Finally, it must be understood that a change in the nomination process has a direct bearing on federalism. David Truman suggests that American federalism does not depend only on the existence of the states or on the states as electoral units for the Senate. He asserts that there is an interrelationship between the political parties and federal constitutional forms and that the link is the parties' nomination

39. *Ibid.*, p. 182.

function. With the rise of the convention system came "an increase in the importance of localism in the selecting process."[40] Originally the presidential candidates were chosen by a congressional caucus dominated by a homogeneous and nationally oriented elite. Truman believes that "the shift of initiative to the state legislatures and later to the national delegate conventions was a response to demands from more heterogeneous elements in the population and eventuated in a shifting of the power of decision, if not the initiative from the national to the state or local level."[41]

The true link between individual state parties is the President-nominating process. No aspirant can hope to be a candidate unless he forms a coalition of state and local parties. In consequence, the states play an influential role in the selection of the President. What begins at the nominating level carries over to the campaign. The states are the decisive units. All other units—the cities, the counties, the various interest groups—are important to the campaign strategists in terms of the voting combinations that can be formed to win statewide pluralities. Because a candidate must carry states, he will often commit himself to issues crucial to the states. Under a direct-election system, state boundaries would lose their significance and state and local issues would be neglected by the candidates. According to David Derge, the direct election would not only have a na-

40. David B. Truman, "Federalism and the Party System," in *Federalism Mature and Emergent*, ed. Arthur W. MacMahon (New York, 1955), p. 119.
   41. *Ibid.*

tionalizing effect on the issues of the presidential campaign, but this nationalizing effect would extend to all elections tied to the presidential race.

The nationalization of the presidential issues is an obvious result, particularly as candidates look beyond the "big" 12 States for their votes and grope to connect with existing or latent groups whose membership spills over State lines. It seems likely that anyone running for office would be pulled into this vortex of national issues and could hardly avoid taking his stand on the ones which prove effective for the presidential nominees. Since these issues would probably be both transcendant and dramatic, legitimate State and local issues might fare even more poorly than they sometimes do now.[42]

The electioneering muscle of the state parties might atrophy if the states were no longer the decisive political units. The national party organizations might not benefit, though the presidential candidate and his campaign apparatus probably would. Instead of having his constituencies imposed upon him in state-sized packages, the candidate would be much freer to select his own constituencies, to organize units from groups that spill over state lines. If so, private groups could be politicized as partial substitutes for the state party organizations as electioneering tools for the presidential campaign.

In the composition of the national government, in the terms of Herbert Wechsler, "the states are the strategic yardsticks for the measurement of interest and opinion, the special centers of political activity, the separate geographi-

42. 1968 Senate *Hearings*, p. 633.

cal determinants of national as well as local politics."[43] The result is that the drive for the Presidency is a drive for wide support. Although all the possible changes under a direct-election system cannot be foreseen, the potential for disturbance of federalism has not been sufficiently considered by either the Senate or the House in their hearings and debates. The prospect of a nationalization of issues and of a reduction in the power and influence of the state parties in both the nominating and the electioneering processes has not been examined.

According to Congressman Celler, "the provisions for a national runoff election in the proposed new article which we have offered are not merely collateral to the direct election plan; they are an essential part in confining potential splinter parties and their candidates."[44] The provision for a popular runoff is an integral part of the entire reform. The questions are: Would this reform eliminate or add to the uncertainties surrounding an election? Would it promote or prevent a national crisis? The direct-election process would abolish the unit rule, and the reformers decided that something must take its place if the country was to avoid the mire of two national elections, of a general election transformed into a national primary followed by a runoff. Their plan was to design a contingency procedure which would prevent a splintering of the vote and forestall runoffs. Yet that procedure would do the opposite.

43. "Political Safeguards of Federalism," in *Principles, Politics and Fundamental Law* (Cambridge, Mass., 1961), p. 54.

44. *Congressional Record*, Vol. 115, Pt. 19, 91st Cong., 1st sess. (1969), p. 25983.

We now have a single election; we now have a viable two-party system; we now have a national-convention system which presents us with well-qualified candidates. These are strong reasons why we should scrape the barnacles off our present electoral system, not scuttle it.

4 Inequalities in Voting Power

In the early 1960's the Supreme Court, in its reapportionment decisions, articulated the principle of "one man, one vote." This principle has had a profound effect on the direction of electoral-college reform. Although the principle has since been applied to a variety of elections, the Court cannot extend it to the constitutionally instituted electoral college. So the politicians have taken this task upon themselves.

Because the electoral-count system creates advantages for some voters and discriminates against others, it directly contradicts the principle of one man, one vote. It gives an advantage to intrastate majority and plurality voters; to voters in large states (though some continue to claim that voters in small states benefit more); to tightly organized, highly disciplined special-interest groups in large, urban states; to voters in states that are losing population; and finally, to voters in low-turnout states.

Many critics base their objections to the present system on the argument that every citizen has a right to an equally weighted vote. Thus they argue it is incumbent on the Congress and the states to amend the Constitution to give every voter an equally weighted vote in presidential elections. In reply, those who would not scrap the system contend that the Supreme Court's one man, one vote principle has sloganized and trivialized the democratic process. Irving Kristol and Paul Weaver argue that "far from being a complex idea, implying a complex mode of government appropriate to a large and complex society, the idea of democracy has been debased into a simple-minded arithmetical majoritarianism—government by adding-machine."[1]

The voting-weight advantages are tied to the unit rule and to the geographic subdivisions of the presidential constituency. Alternative reform proposals which would continue these two practices have been rejected by the critics as undemocratic and even "unconstitutional." "There is only one system which guarantees that the basic principle of our Constitution—one man, one vote—will be carried forth in the selection of our Chief Executive. There is only one system that treats all Americans equally. That system is direct election."[2] The one man, one vote slogan has attracted a great following, and it may come as a shock to many that the Constitution says no such thing. The Supreme Court, not the Constitution, laid down this doctrine, and as Alexander Bickel has pointed out, we are now being asked to "amend the Constitution to make it mean what the Supreme Court has said it means."[3] The question is, Should we?

1. "A Bad Idea Whose Time Has Come," *New York Times Magazine*, Nov. 23, 1969, p. 43.
2. Statement of Congressman Abner Mikva, *Congressional Record*, Vol. 115, Pt. 19, 91st Cong., 1st sess. (1969), p. 25158.
3. *The New Age of Political Reform* (New York, 1968), p. 10.

First let us examine the case against the present system. The population does vary in size and distribution from one decennial census to another, and thus the voters in states with declining populations or with populations that grow at a rate below the national average have a temporary advantage over the voters in states with increasing populations. However, neither our state nor our national government is designed to be immediately or fully responsive to population shifts. The Senate has a fixed apportionment and the House is apportioned according to the decennial census. And since, under the Constitution, each state is awarded as many electoral votes as it has senators and representatives, a state's electoral-college strength and its congressional strength are cut from the same cloth. The direct-election plan would make alterations in the President's electoral vestments, which were tailored to fit the congressional representation accorded each state.

Election by the constituency of the whole, a constituency undistorted by an outdated decennial apportionment, could give the President a political advantage over the Congress. The President would have an additional argument—that he represented an up-to-date constituency—to support his claim to speak most authentically for the people. This would be an additional argument because the reform would make him the only national officer (except for the Vice-President) directly elected by the people. A claim for a more authentic mandate than that possessed by the Congress begins right there. Alfred de Grazia believes the "constituency of the whole is important politically if only because the officer acquires a large increment of prestige and authority from expressing sometimes the desires and sentiments of the collectivity of voters."[4]

The political ramifications of each decennial census are extensive. Any basic change in the congressional apportionment may affect to some degree a state's voting power in the national nominating conventions. Furthermore, it may well affect the state's share in the fruits of presidential victory. It may change the political balance of a state's delegation in the Congress and even the internal power structure of the Congress. A state can lose more than a representative; it can lose a representative with seniority on a key committee. However, in a study of the national implications of congressional reapportionment, David Farrelly and Ivan Hinderaker suggest that "even if all the factors contributing to national political power were measurable, the changes produced by any one decennial reapportionment of congressional seats are usually slight."[5]

The effect on presidential elections is apparently also slight. Even though a change in the electoral-vote apportionment could change the campaign strategy, it would appear that the distortion resulting from an outdated apportionment has not been as serious in terms of the presidential contest as anticipated. For example, if in the 1940 Franklin Roosevelt–Wendell Willkie election the 1941 apportionment had been used, the result would probably have been four more electoral votes for Roosevelt and four fewer for

4. "General Theory of Apportionment," *Law and Contemporary Problems* 17 (1952), 257.

5. "Congressional Reapportionment and National Political Power," *Law and Contemporary Problems* 17 (1952), 339.

Willkie. In the 1941 reapportionment nine states lost and seven gained electoral votes. The only state to gain more than one electoral vote was California, which acquired three more. Yet California was already a top-priority state with twenty-two electoral votes. And Illinois, Ohio, Massachusetts, and Pennsylvania, which lost one vote each, also were big electoral-vote prizes. Thus the campaign strategy would not have been seriously affected.

In 1948, Truman's margin over Dewey would have been increased by four electoral votes if the election had been run under the 1951 apportionment. Again the only state whose position changed appreciably was California, which gained seven votes, but even according to the old apportionment California was the fourth-ranking state in the union in terms of electoral strength and was a highly competitive state to boot. In 1960, Kennedy would still have defeated Nixon, but by a smaller margin, if the election had been run under the 1961 apportionment. Kennedy would have lost approximately ten electoral votes. Again California, then the second-ranking state, was the big gainer, winning eight electoral votes. Florida followed, with a gain of four. New York, Pennsylvania, Illinois, and Massachusetts all lost electoral votes but not enough to detract from their appeal as big prizes.

Since electoral votes are allotted, in the main, by population and not by the actual numbers of voters, voters in low-turnout states have an advantage over those in high-turnout states. In 1968 the voters who derived the greatest advantage from a low turnout lived in six southern states and the District of Columbia, whose turnout was 10 percent below the national average. These voters influenced 14 percent of the electoral vote. Nixon won twenty electoral votes in these states, Humphrey twenty-eight, and Wallace twenty-nine. The following figures for the low-turnout states, drawn from the 1970 *World Almanac*, give the number of electoral votes and the percentage of the population of voting age that cast ballots for President in 1968.

State	Electoral votes	Percent turnout
Ala.	10	50.3
D.C.	3	33.5
Ga.	12	42.9
Miss.	7	50.6
S.C.	8	45.9
Tex.	25	48.5
Va.	12	50.4

Those voters who were at the greatest disadvantage because their states had a turnout 10 percent higher than the national average lived in five states of the interior and influenced 6 percent of the electoral vote. Twenty of their electoral votes went to Nixon and ten to Humphrey. The following figures are for the high-turnout states.

State	Electoral votes	Percent turnout
Idaho	4	72.6
Ind.	13	71.8
Minn.	10	76.0
S.D.	4	72.8
Utah	4	76.1

One critic of the present system, Neal Peirce, does not seem overly concerned about this vote distortion, because he finds the media are nationalizing presidential politics and two-party competition is increasing throughout the nation. He believes we are "fast approaching the day when there will be no appreciable difference between voter turnouts in the various states."[6] The statistics support Peirce's conclusion; the discrepancy in voter turnout has narrowed since 1920. In 1920 the first-ranking state in voter turnout was Kentucky, with 71.2 percent, and the lowest-ranking state was South Carolina, with 8.6 percent. The difference between them was 62.6 percent. In 1968 the highest-ranking state was Utah, with 76.1 percent, and the lowest-ranking was Georgia, with 42.9 percent. The difference between the two was 33.2 percent. In 1920 the average turnout was 44.2 percent, and in 1968 it was 61 percent. There has been a significant increase nationally in voter turnout in the past fifty years, and only two states had lower turnouts in 1968 than they did in 1920. The turnout percentage has not, however, increased uniformly throughout the nation but has increased most markedly in those states which in 1920 had very low participation percentages. The average 1968 increase over the turnout in 1920 was 17.7 percent, but the average 1968 increase in the eight states with the lowest turnout in 1920 was 33.9 percent.

Richard M. Scammon believes that a direct election

6. U.S., Senate, Committee on the Judiciary, Subcommittee on Constitutional Amendments, *Hearings, Election of the President,* 89th Cong., 2d sess., and 90th Cong., 1st sess., 1968, p. 235 (cited hereafter as 1968 Senate *Hearings*).

would increase voter turnout, because every voter would know that his vote would be counted directly in the choice. He argues that our elections would therefore be more democratic, because voter participation would be increased.[7] This may be true, but given the evidence of the Survey Research Center, the increase in voter turnout would not be as large as is anticipated. The Survey Research Center, at the University of Michigan, according to Donald Stokes, found that a voter who has a strong preference or who believes the *national* race is close is more likely to vote. But the closeness of the race in his own state does not affect his participation. Stokes concludes that "the voter generally seems to miss the fact of the unit rule."[8] An increased turnout under the direct-election plan could be expected only if, in fact, the voters are aware of the state unit rule and if, further, this knowledge affects their present voting habits. The evidence is that these assumptions are unwarranted.

The apparent concern of most reformers is voter equality, and they frame their case against the present system in terms of disadvantaged and disfranchised voters. Harvey Zeidenstein suggests that those who vote for the intrastate minority-party candidate are disfranchised because the unit rule gives the entire electoral vote to the winner of the statewide plurality. As he interprets it, the unit rule adds insult to injury because the votes for the intrastate losing candidate are not only "lost" but are added to those of the winning candidate. His interpretation derives from what he terms "simple generic differences" between the office

7. *Ibid.*, p. 579.
8. *Ibid.*, p. 569.

sought and the votes for that office. He is quite right when he says that "so long as one's vote is *counted for the candidate of one's choice*, that vote is not 'lost.' "[9] The fact is that under the unit rule the votes are so counted in each state. If and when they are not, it is because of fraud, which no electoral system can completely prevent. If one voted for the McGovern electors in the state of New York in 1972, one's vote was counted for the McGovern electors. The votes were counted for the offices that were to be filled, but the office in question was not, as Zeidenstein seems to assume, the office of President, but rather the office of presidential elector. As long as the votes for this or any other office are honestly and accurately counted for the office to be filled, the votes are not lost. The problem lies in his assumption that the office to be filled should be that of the President.

His effort to make a distinction between divisible electoral votes and the office sought as an indivisible prize overlooks the fact that an office is also divisible in terms of time and function. Both the votes and the office are potentially divisible, and the basic question is not whether they are divisible but whether they should be. Joseph Dolan agrees, suggesting that this kind of argument "is like saying a man has lost his dinner after it has been completely digested." Dolan finds the lost-vote argument fallacious because in any election, even a direct election, those who vote for the losing candidate have "lost" their votes unless we "provide that if the Republican candidate gets 55 percent of the vote

9. Harvey Zeidenstein, *Direct Election of the President* (Lexington, Mass., 1973), pp. 6–7.

and the Democratic candidate gets 45 percent, the Republican shall be President 55 percent of the year and the Democrat for the remaining time."[10] We do not divide offices in this way because, among other things, of the desirability of unity and stability. Zeidenstein apparently has no quarrel with the federal principle as a jurisdictional basis for electing the national legislature, though if we abandoned the principle, the national legislature would more accurately reflect the preferences of individual voters and the congressional majority party would not be overrepresented, as it usually is. If the values associated with federalism and geographical jurisdictions still exist for the legislature, why, precisely, should we abandon them for the executive? The argument that the federal principle offends intrastate voter equality does not hold, for voters within each state are treated equally as long as their votes are counted for the candidate of their choice within their state. The issue is not intrastate voter equality but, rather, the validity of federalism as a condition on national elections. But the case against federalism has not been made. Federalism, it must be remembered, looks to a certain form of political majority as appropriate to a large, heterogeneous, pluralistic nation. It looks to the formation of concurrent, not arithmetical, majorities.

The same argument applies to that intrastate "majority" composed of all those who did not vote for the plurality candidate. The charges of intrastate voter inequalities are

10. "How We Elect Our President: An Electoral College Education in One Lesson," *American Bar Association Journal* 42 (1956), 1038,

rather empty technicalities if we consider our long history of electoral victories for the national plurality winner, unless the real aim of reform is a realignment of the power structure. And in fact this may be the issue; though the debate is often framed in terms of establishing national arithmetical majorities, for many the real object is to realign the political majorities. Their concern is not that the votes for the losing candidate in any state are "lost" or given to the winner of the statewide plurality but, rather, that certain interest and partisan groups cannot combine their votes across state lines effectively and, as a result, have less influence on candidate and issue selection and campaign strategy than groups that can combine their votes across state lines. Under a direct-election system the geographical barriers would be destroyed and the power structure realigned.

Despite the principle of voter equality proclaimed by the Supreme Court, the electoral-reform issue is a power struggle. Time and again the critics of the present system and its defenders have abandoned theoretical debate and framed their objections in terms of practical consequences. Senator John Stennis was aroused by the fact that under the present system the balance of power has swung to the population centers of the large industrial states and that now "the eleven largest states and any one other state have a sufficient number of electoral votes to carry the presidential election."[11] Senator George Smathers complained that "the present system adds weight and strength to minority controlled groups far beyond their numbers."[12] The direct-

11. 1968 Senate *Hearings*, p. 77.
12. *Ibid.*, p. 268.

election plan impressed Senator Bayh because it would "give the opportunity to the candidates to go into all areas of the country, to stress the national aspect of the campaign rather than concentrate on a few large areas which now yield so much power in the final determination."[13] In an interview conducted by the *Congressional Quarterly*, he pointed out that, in 1968, when the Humphrey forces wrote off Indiana "it demoralized the grass roots strength of our party."[14] Congressman William Clay is opposed to direct election because it "would inhibit the political influence of minority groups" and in particular the black vote, which he believes is "more effectively applied with the two party system which has evolved from the electoral college."[15] Congressman Edward Boland, who supported direct election, believes that "there would be less need than at present for the major parties to make excessive concessions to minority groups who may hold the balance of power in certain states."[16] The debate is not simply on political equality in the abstract; the debate is on the locus of power. Where should presidential elections be decided? Which forces should be strengthened, which weakened?

The clearest indication of this power struggle is found in the small-state–large-state argument. Which states have the advantage in voting power under both the present and proposed systems is a matter of some importance, because

13. *Ibid.*, p. 363.
14. *Congressional Quarterly* 28 (April 17, 1970), 1027.
15. *Congressional Record*, Vol. 115, Pt. 19, 91st Cong., 1st sess. (1969), p. 25390.
16. 1968 Senate *Hearings*, p. 80.

the small states have the power to reject an amendment. Only thirteen states are needed for rejection, and at present fifteen states have fewer than five electoral votes.

There has been long-standing confusion on the question of whether the small or the large states have the advantage. The bonus votes would appear to give the small states an advantage. Initially the movement for electoral reform was supported by the small states and the less populous regions, which saw that candidates, issues, and campaign strategies were selected with the large populous states in mind. Awareness of neglect led them to press for reforms that would retain the electoral college but abolish the unit rule. Some political analysts are convinced that if the electoral college is retained without the unit rule, the advantage would fall to the small states.[17] The district and proportional plans and the Mundt-Daniel hybrid that offered the states a choice of either have lost support largely because they would change the present power alignments in favor of the small states.

John F. Banzhaf's study gives the mathematical case for the present advantage to the large states. He set out to measure voting power, the individual voter's ability to affect the outcome by his vote. The number of voting combinations in which an individual can alter the outcome by

17. John F. Banzhaf III, "One Man, 3.312 Votes: A Mathematical Analysis of the Electoral College," *Villanova Law Review* 13 (Winter 1968), p. 304; Allan P. Sindler, "Presidential Election Methods and Urban-Ethnic Interests," *Law and Contemporary Problems* 27 (1962), 213; John H. Yunker and Lawrence D. Longley, "The Biases of the Electoral College," in Donald R. Matthews, ed., *Perspectives on Presidential Selection* (Washington, 1973), pp. 172–203.

changing his vote is Banzhaf's measure of voting power. According to his calculations the New Yorker has a relative voting power of 3.312, and the Alaskan a relative voting power of 1.838.[18]

The reason for this inequality in favor of the large States is that all of the States' electoral votes go to the candidate with the plurality. Although a New Yorker has fewer votes per unit of population than a resident of a smaller State, he has the potential for influencing through his vote, a very large block of electoral votes. In this case the mathematics clearly shows that the ability to affect a large block of electoral votes more than offsets the disadvantages of having less electoral votes per unit of population.[19]

This thesis is supported by the histories of presidential campaigns and by the fact that the candidates have been overwhelmingly citizens from the large states. Banzhaf calculates that in a direct election every voter in every state would have the same voting power. Although this mathematical analysis explains a widely recognized political reality, the belief persists in some quarters that the small states have a great voting-power advantage under the present system which they would lose under a direct-election method.

In the 1968 Senate hearings, Senator Spessard Holland presented a table comparing each state's percentage of the population to its percentage of the electoral votes to support his argument that under the direct-election plan thirty-

18. Banzhaf, "Mathematical Analysis of the Electoral College," p. 329.

19. U.S., House of Representatives, Committee on the Judiciary, *Hearings, Electoral College Reform*, 91st Cong., 1st sess., 1969, p. 353 (cited hereafter as 1969 House *Hearings*).

two states would be losers. His calculations indicate that New York and California would be the greatest gainers. New York's population percentage in 1960 was 9.4, and its electoral-vote percentage was 8. The conclusion is that New York would gain 1.4 percent. On the other hand, Alaska had a population percentage of 0.1 and an electoral-vote percentage of 0.5. Thus it would lose 0.4 percent. According to Senator Holland's table the thirteen large states presently have an electoral-vote percentage smaller than their population percentage, and the thirty-two smaller states and the District of Columbia have an electoral-vote percentage larger than their population percentage. The direct election would abolish the unit rule, a reform for which the small states have pressed. But it also would abolish the bonus votes. Senator Holland fears this undesirable reform.

Senator Carl Curtis of Nebraska, who concurs with Senator Holland's analysis, told a *Congressional Quarterly* interviewer: "My state of Nebraska has 92/100ths of 1 percent of the electoral vote. Based on the last election we had 73/100ths of 1 percent of the popular vote. I'm not authorized to reduce the voting power of my state by 20 percent. The legislatures will not ratify it."[20] If there were a simple relationship between the electoral votes per unit of population and voting power, this analysis might have more force (though one may wonder how intensely the states would feel the loss of 20/100ths of 1 percent). The electoral-count system may appear to give an advantage to the

20. *Congressional Quarterly*, 28 (April 17, 1970), 1028.

small states by awarding them the bonus votes. But the political reality is that the unit rule has not only compensated for that advantage; it has also created one for the large states.

This is only the beginning of the tale, for it is not the large states simply that have the greatest advantage, but the large doubtful states. Banzhaf's study calculated the individual voter's power to affect the outcome of the contest by his act on election day. As Banzhaf points out, his was a study of theoretical, not of actual, voting power because it did not consider such factors as the relative power of political parties within the states or the psychology of the individual voter, who may decide to cast a protest vote for a third-party candidate.[21] Thus the voter in Texas, with its twenty-five electoral votes, had, in 1968, according to his calculations, a relative voting power of 2.452, and the voter in Ohio, with its twenty-six electoral votes, had a relative voting power of 2.539. The difference is only .087 percent, yet any national politician knows that Ohio has been one of the major electoral battle grounds, and until very recently Texas has not. Texas has been an upperclassman in the electoral college since the turn of the century, in 1900 ranking sixth in the number of electoral votes. But Texas has been a stalwartly Democratic state. Of the eighteen elections from 1900 to 1968, Texas Democrats have won fifteen. And, with the exception of 1928, the Texas Democrats have won by great margins (70 to 30 or 80 to 20) until the "native-son" Eisenhower victory in 1952. On the

21. Banzhaf, "Mathematical Analysis of the Electoral College," p. 308.

other hand, Ohio gave seven of the eighteen elections to the Democrats and eleven to the Republicans. While neither party won elections by huge margins, there were five hairbreadth contests in which the margin was as little as 0.2 percent.

Ohio is a doubtful state where each major party has seen a real chance of victory. Although the majority party is careful to observe all the political amenities in a large state which provides lopsided majorities, it does not woo and court the voters in such states with the same passion it directs toward the voters in large competitive states. The direct election would take away the advantage that competitive Ohio has had over noncompetitive Texas.

Under a direct-election system, state lines would no longer be barriers preventing minority voters in Illinois and Arkansas from combining their votes with those of their persuasion in Indiana. The states would no longer be the decisive political units in the election. State lines would not, however, be totally irrelevant, if only because the states presumably would continue to count the votes (state tallies might still provide convenient statistics for election analysis) and the state parties would continue to have some electioneering function. If only the popular votes were counted, the large states would still have considerable influence, because of the sheer number of their voters. But their influence would be reduced, because they no longer could supply the huge blocs of electoral votes which give them great control over candidate and issue selection under the unit rule. Their competitiveness would no longer augment their power in the councils of the national parties.

At the same time the direct-election plan would change the status of noncompetitive states. One of the frequent complaints against the present system is that it tends to perpetuate one-party states, because the minority party "loses" all of its votes under the unit rule. The reformers believe that under a direct election the second party would bestir itself to compaign vigorously in one-party states, since the votes won by its efforts would apply to the national tally.[22] Under the present system, however, there are two kinds of wasted votes: those wasted because they do not constitute part of a statewide plurality, and those wasted because they are vastly in excess of the statewide plurality needed for victory. Polsby and Wildavsky believe that under a direct election the real incentive for increased partisan activity in a one-party state falls to the majority party, not the minority party.[23] When the unit rule is in effect, it is of no advantage to a candidate to poll 60, 70, or 80 percent of the vote in one-party states. The huge margins are wasted, since no electoral-vote bonuses are given for winning a state by a landslide. As a result, one-party states are often neglected by both major parties. The votes of the statewide majority party are taken for granted, and those of the minority party are discounted because they do not yield electoral votes. Under a direct-election system one-party states would take on a new importance if state party leaders could

22. Statement of Congressman Edward Boland, *Congressional Record*, Vol. 115, Pt. 18, 91st Cong., 1st sess. (1969), p. 24977.

23. Nelson Polsby and Aaron Wildavsky, *Presidential Elections: Strategies of American Electoral Politics* (New York, 1960), pp. 244–245.

increase the turnout and provide the largest possible margins of victory in a close election.

At present the 26 electoral votes of competitive Illinois are vigorously fought over, whereas the 10 of noncompetitive Louisiana are not. But in a close popular election in which the winner's national margin might be a few hundred thousand votes, Louisiana would take on a new importance if it provided the winner with a 170,000 vote margin and Illinois yielded only a 9,000 vote margin. By ranking the large states and the southern states in order of the margin of the votes given to the winner of the state in the close election of 1960, Polsby and Wildavsky discovered that "ten of the eleven Southern states exceeded the large states of Illinois, California and New Jersey in popular vote margins." They conclude that since the emphasis would be "on the *difference* in the popular vote between the two candidates," one-party states, which can turn out large majorities with greater ease than two-party states, would take on a new importance in the minds of candidates and campaign strategists.[24] They therefore suggest that the "reformers are attempting to do away with the very system which helps to prevent the election of the President by one-party states."[25] Their argument is supported by Yunker and Longley, who, in an extension of Banzhaf's study, also found that the South was at a disadvantage under the electoral-college system.[26]

Instead of being ignored by the candidates and the cam-

24. *Ibid.*
25. *Ibid.*, p. 246.
26. "Biases of the Electoral College," p. 193.

paign managers, the smaller homogeneous states would probably command attention when their huge margins of victory can be the decisive factor in a close election; and the state party leaders whose efforts increase party turnout would be rewarded. A host of benefits flows to those who hold strategic positions during the election of a President. Among the rewards which parties distribute on a quid-pro-quo basis are the appointive federal offices, including Cabinet and Supreme Court nominations. Under the present system these fruits of victory fall to the large pivotal states. Between 1900 and 1968, New York won 33 out of 168 Cabinet appointments; Pennsylvania, 12; Illinois, 12; Massachusetts, 11; and Ohio, 9. Fifteen states did not win one Cabinet appointment, and eleven states have had only one. If Polsby and Wildavsky are correct, state party leaders in states that provide wide margins of victory would share in the spoils of victory, and this could result in a seriously overweighted position for the one-party states, which through the seniority and committee systems already wield vast power in the Congress.

Another belief about the large-state–small-state advantage has been called the urban-ethnic hypothesis. Because seven of the eight largest cities (New York, Chicago, Los Angeles, Philadelphia, Detroit, Houston, and Cleveland) are situated in the states with the greatest number of electoral votes, and because, according to Banzhaf's calculations, citizens in large states have voting-power advantages over those in smaller states, some analysts believe urban-ethnic voters enjoy a special advantage under the electoral-college system. To test this hypothesis, Yunker and Longley extended Banzhaf's study to the average voting power of various demographic groups and compared it with the average voting power of the whole population. "Large states, metropolitan area residents (including residents of central cities, SMSAs [standard metropolitan statistical areas], and especially suburbs), population of foreign stock, blue-collar workers, and the regions of the Far West and the East were found to be advantaged by the electoral college."[27] They conclude that the "data seem to confirm the urban-ethnic hypothesis at least in the aggregate sense." They found only two possible exceptions: (1) blacks have less than average voting power because of their high concentrations in small and medium-sized states, as well as in the central cities of large states; and (2) suburban residents are slightly more advantaged than residents of the central cities, though they note that the central cities have greater than average voting power.[28]

Both Yunker and Longley are well aware of the limitations of pivotal-voting-power studies, particularly in terms of voter and candidate perceptions and the relative degrees of voter influence on issue positions and policy direction. The effect of voter groups on issue selection, policy positions, and even candidate selection may be a function of many variables, such as degree of organization, visibility, levels of political activity, as well as strategic location. Thus, under the electoral-count system the balance of power in the large competitive states may go to tightly organized, highly disciplined groups in large urban areas.

27. *Ibid.*, p. 202.
28. *Ibid.*, p. 193.

This is not to say that they always are decisive in terms of the outcome of the contest, but rather that they are formidable blocs that can be ignored or offended at a candidate's peril. Nor is it to say that there are no limits on the ability of a minority-group leader to swing his bloc from one candidate to another. Clearly there are such limits, particularly in the stability of partisan preferences. Angus Campbell and the Survey Research Center have found the "lasting attachment of tens of millions of Americans to one of the parties" a very important factor in national elections.[29] Within limits, the parties have some room to maneuver. Rarely does any minority bloc vote unanimously for one party or another. But there appears to be a normal voting pattern for each of them. A pattern can be altered favorably if a party selects candidates and issues that are highly appealing to a group. It can be altered unfavorably if a party selects candidates and issues hostile to a group.

It is a fact of modern coalition politics that urban minorities have a demonstrable partisan preference: they usually vote for the Democratic candidate. If, however, a party chooses a candidate who is perceived either as vastly more favorable or as more hostile to a group's vital interests, that group's percentage for its traditional favorite may be affected. Voters in such groups may be called "swing" voters, not in the sense that individual voters quickly or easily change their electoral support from one party to another, but rather in the sense that they may have an effect on a close election because the group greatly increases its turn-

29. Angus Campbell *et al.*, *The American Voter* (New York, 1964), p. 67.

out and improves its solidity for its traditional favorite or the reverse. In a close election dramatic changes in a group's support for its traditional favorite may tip the balance of victory in large competitive states, particularly when the group's vote is concentrated in such states rather than dissipated throughout the nation. That such dramatic changes occur is demonstrated by history.

Democratic voters among nonwhites ranged from 61 percent in 1956 to 94 percent in 1964. Nonwhites also registered an 87 percent vote for McGovern in 1972. From 1952 to 1968, the Democratic vote among Jews ranged from 75 percent in 1956 to 81 percent in 1961, with about 60 percent voting Democratic in 1972. . . . The percentage of Catholics who voted Democratic ranges from 51 percent in 1956 to 78 percent in 1960, but dipped to 48 percent in 1972. Finally, members of labor union families voted Democratic by percentages ranging from 56 percent in 1968 to 73 percent in 1964, with 46 percent voting for McGovern in 1972.[30]

Because the large competitive states have an electoral advantage and because some minority blocs are concentrated in these states, "modern Presidents have been especially sensitive and responsive to urban and minority interests."[31] It is not so much that these competitive-state minority blocs are urban or liberal, but that they are self-conscious, well organized, and strategically located. Because they are well organized, they are alert to policies that affect their interests. They have the manpower and machinery to activate their members. Among the favored minority groups, the

30. Zeidenstein, *Direct Election*, p. 28.
31. Statement of Alexander Bickel, 1969 House *Hearings*, p. 411.

labor unions have used their organizational machinery with great skill and effectiveness. In the 1968 campaign the unions had a great impact, although their candidate, Hubert Humphrey, eventually lost. According to Theodore H. White, their unprecedented effort sharply reduced Wallace's draw on the workers. "In the near miracle of the Humphrey comeback in October, no single factor was more important than the army of organized labor, roused to the greatest political exertion of its history."[32]

In some cases the leaders of minority groups are able to swing votes so as to increase their blocs' percentage for a given candidate, particularly if one candidate is perceived as a particular friend of their interests and the other is not. But often it is not so much a matter of swinging some group members away from their traditional partisan preferences as of bringing out the group vote. An organized minority which believes that its interests are threatened will throng to the polls, marshaled and prodded by its leaders. Members of these groups do have long-standing partisan attachments, like the rest of us. Their votes are not simply up for bid, with the best offer winning the day. Instead, they obtain a generally satisfactory response from both parties, because the party which is not their traditional favorite wants to preclude a strenuous all-out effort in opposition. Sometimes it is simply a matter of letting sleeping dogs lie.

The special position of some minority groups under the present system is a function of their uneven national dis-

32. Theodore H. White, *The Making of the President, 1968* (New York, 1969), p. 365.

tribution. The fact that Jews, blacks, and Catholics are disproportionately located in states which provide large blocs of electoral votes makes them strategically important. In 1960, Kennedy's Catholicism was a two-edged sword which, considered nationally, cut both ways, but considered in terms of electoral votes was an advantage, because the main body of the Catholic vote was located in the large competitive states most of which Kennedy won by small margins. Despite the tug of partisan attachments, the religious issue provoked shifts in voting patterns. Kennedy was hurt by these shifts in the South, the Border States, and some parts of the Midwest, but he was helped in the North and in the large industrial states of the Midwest. The result was a net advantage for Kennedy on the issue of his religion.[33]

This is not to say that the Catholic vote gave him the election or that all "these groups can shift their votes more rapidly than other groups in the population."[34] The anti-Catholic vote shift was significant, but it was not strategically located. As a number of election analysts have suggested, in any election in which the popular vote is close several groups may claim that their support was crucial. The parties cannot identify with scientific accuracy the locus of the votes that made the difference between victory and defeat. But this means that they will be sensitive to all the groups whose claim is plausible, not that they will be

33. Polsby and Wildavsky, *Presidential Elections,* p. 21.
34. Neal Peirce, *The People's President: The Electoral College in American History and the Direct Vote Alternative* (New York, 1968), p. 282.

sensitive to none of them. In 1960 the Gallup poll reported that the Jews increased their Democratic vote by 6 percent over the 1956 election, and the blacks by 7 percent. Because Kennedy won states like Illinois and Texas by relatively small margins, both these minority groups could claim to have made the difference. The combined electoral vote of these two states is 51, or 9 percent of the entire number. Whether the Jews and blacks actually had a crucial effect is beside the point. If the parties think they might have, they are going to take these groups into consideration.

Samuel Rabinove, writing in the monthly Jewish review *Midstream*, notes that under the direct-election plan "the existing strategic location of Jewish voters would become utterly meaningless."[35] There are approximately 6,000,000 Jews in the country, and more than 70 percent of them live in the seven large industrial states that have the most electoral votes. In New York, in 1969, the Jews made up 14 percent of the statewide population. A candidate perceived to be hostile to the interests of the Jewish community in New York has little chance of winning that state, because the parties there are closely divided. By repealing the unit rule which creates their strategic position, the direct election "would result in a diminution of Jewish political influence."[36] This is precisely what some of the advocates of reform have in mind. Whether minority leverage in presidential contests should be sacrificed on the altar of purist

35. "The Electoral College Enigma," *Midstream*, June–July 1969, p. 53.
36. *Ibid.*

democracy is another question, a question which can only be answered in the context of the whole governmental power system.

Those who discount the special position of urban minority groups argue that even if they were to concede that these groups have an advantage, "it is not clear that it would always be liberals who enjoy the special advantage."[37] This surely is true. Much of the appeal of the Kennedy counterweight argument did arise from the fact that urban and liberal interests have coincided in our recent history. The counterweight argument, however, did not stand on liberalism alone but also on urbanism. Alexander Bickel argued that "the urban outlook and interest on the one hand, and the rural-small town outlook and interest on the other, do generally differ."[38] In the Congress, according to the counterweight argument, the rural–small-town outlook and interest have generally prevailed. The conservative and the rural–small-town outlook often coincide, as do the urban and liberal. Neither correlation is cast in bronze. For example, the Progressive movement sprouted and flourished in the rural West and Midwest. But as long as urban and rural interests differ, and as long as the Congress is sensitive to one, it does not seem unreasonable that the Presidency should be sensitive to the other. Furthermore, the great urban centers are the areas where the most pressing problems usually develop first. It matters less that the liberals can claim these problems as their special concern and project than that they are urgent and potentially explosive.

37. Peirce, *People's President*, p. 282.
38. 1969 House *Hearings*, p. 412.

The overstrained welfare system, public employees' strikes, racial tensions, the rising crime rate, air and water pollution, while all problems of national concern, are most grave and importunate in the urban centers. The urban areas must have access to the national power structure, and the President's special sensitivity to their needs may be a blessing, for many of these problems must be handled from a national perspective. The President, whose function may be to balance the localism and the separatism of the Congress, can initiate programs that attack these problems nationally.

But the reformers insist that the old order is passing and a new one is arising which will change the nature of the Congress. In the early 1960's the Supreme Court's reapportionment decisions appeared to have struck a fatal blow at the rural-conservative bias of the Congress. The reformers insist the counterweight argument has been successfully rebutted. But has it? Can the Congress be radically changed by reapportionment?

Alexander Bickel points out some of the most formidable barriers against a substantive change in the Congress.[39] Short of a constitutional amendment, neither the House, where each state is guaranteed at least one representative, nor the Senate can be changed to give each voter an equal voice in the composition of the Congress. And in the case of the Senate even a constitutional amendment might not serve, since according to Article V no state can be deprived of equal representation in the Senate without its consent. Furthermore, as long as the nation uses the decennial cen-

39. Bickel, *New Age*, p. 11.

sus, population shifts will result in distortions in individual voting power for congressmen. And as long as we use the single-member-district system in selecting members of the House, distortions will flow from variations in district voter turnout. Arithmetically equal contiguous districts are not necessarily politically fair districts. District lines may cut through some interest groups and not others. Gerrymandering is still possible, because partisan strength is not evenly distributed geographically and the ingenuity of state legislators should not be underestimated. In the final analysis, reapportionment does not rebut the counterweight argument, because the rebuttal attempt stands on the unwarranted assumption that malapportionment creates the existing congressional bias.

We do not begin to know that Congress is what it is because of malapportionment. It is quite probable that in much larger measure the nature of Congress is determined by its internal methods of distributing power—chiefly the seniority and committee systems. These are very solidly entrenched. They reward length of service and expertise. . . . Long tenure is, in turn, most often the gift of a homogeneous district, which will tend also to liberate a Congressman from the varied concerns of a closely divided and diverse constituency. . . . Congress may also, finally, be what it is because a districted constituency will vote differently for a Congressman, from a more restricted and probably more conservative perspective, than when it votes as part of the entire national constituency in Presidential elections.[40]

At the heart of the counterweight argument is the observation that the Congress has a conservative policy bias,

40. *Ibid.*

not that it deviates from political equality per se. Thus the real question is whether reapportionment can change the policy bias of the Congress. Studies of reapportionment in state legislatures do not indicate that significant changes are in the offing. Thomas R. Dye reports that "the policy choices of malapportioned legislatures are not noticeably different from the policy choices of well-apportioned legislatures." His conclusions are "predicated upon the results obtained from analyzing 30 selected measures of public policy in 3 separate fields—education, welfare and taxation."[41] In another state study Richard I. Hofferbert found no positive correlation between malapportionment and conservative policy.[42] And Robert Dixon notes that "there has been surprisingly little empirical proof or even argumentative proof of the supposed 'bad effects' on government and public policy flowing from malapportionment, or the supposed 'good effects' produced by reapportionment."[43] At best the prospect of substantial congressional change as a result of the reapportionment decisions is premature.

Many reformers have no desire to dilute the present influence of urban minority groups on the Presidency. They believe that while minority groups would no longer be able to influence large blocs of electoral votes, they would still have great effect under a direct election because they could

41. "Malapportionment and Public Policy in the States," *Journal of Politics* 27 (1965), 599.

42. "The Relation between Public Policy and Some Structural and Environmental Variables in the American States," *American Political Science Review* 60 (March 1966), 73–83.

43. *Democratic Representation* (New York, 1968), p. 21.

pool their national strength. Yet under a direct-election plan their strength would be in proportion to their numbers, while under the present system it may be greater than their actual numbers. William Clay, a black congressman from Missouri, was not convinced by the argument that a nationally pooled black vote, including the black votes locked in southern one-party states, would be as effective: "I contend that under the direct vote concept the black vote even in the North, would never count. Had the direct vote been in effect in 1968, all of the black votes in the country would have been cancelled by the 9,800,000 votes received by George Wallace."[44]

The total black population over the age of twenty-one in 1968 was estimated at 11,200,000, and the total population over twenty-one at 119,751,000.[45] Thus if the black population voted as a solid bloc, it would, at a maximum, cast 9 to 10 percent of the total popular vote. But the 41 electoral votes of New York alone are close to 8 percent of the total, and the combined electoral votes of Illinois, New Jersey, New York, and the District of Columbia, which all have large urban black communities, make up 16 percent. The potential effectiveness of 11,000,000 black votes in an all-national election may not be as great as that of the black votes now concentrated in the twelve largest cities. Congressman Clay believes that since the electoral-count system offers the blacks their best opportunity for

---

44. *Congressional Record*, Vol. 115, Pt. 19, 91st Cong., 1st sess. (1969), p. 25392.
45. *The World Almanac, 1970* (New York, 1970), p. 55.

political influence, its abolition would encourage black separatist parties.

As long as the voices of minority groups can be heard through the major parties, the incentive for splinter parties will be kept at a minimum. Historical evidence suggests that when a minority's vital interests are not heeded by at least one of the major parties, a third party is founded. The Dixiecrats of 1948 formed a third party because they believed their voices were not heard in the national party council. Robert La Follette, spokesman for the progressives, originally was a candidate for the Republican nomination in 1916, but he was ignored by his party and ran as an independent in 1924. The Free Soil party was formed when both major parties fell under southern influence. Minority groups need some vehicle to express their interests; they must not be isolated and alienated from the two-party system. Ignored minorities can be driven to desperation and to inflexible positions.

Aside from producing shifts in the power of presently contending groups, a single national constituency may result in widespread and unforeseen changes in group formation and the rise of presently limited or politically unawakened groups. David Derge looks for the development of latent and emerging groups from the academic community and the military. "Neither of these has a history of political effectiveness, yet both involve large numbers and have the potential of becoming formidable groups under the direct popular election of the President."[46] The academic commu-

46. Statement of David Derge, 1968 Senate *Hearings*, p. 633.

nity boiled over the war and continues to do so over other issues, emitting a great steam of publicity, but the academic pots are not in the same constituency. They may bubble over and scald elected officials here and there, but their power is dispersed and geographically divided on the national level. A similar division on the national level is true of the military, since servicemen presently vote by absentee ballot. Once members of a single national constituency, they and their families could form a self-conscious group with certain well-defined interests that might attract a candidate's attention.

The present system unquestionably creates some inequalities in individual voting power. But the list of inequalities in voting power compiled by critics of the present system is far from complete. The electoral-count system also discriminates against ideologically extreme voters and parties, sectional and national third parties, and voters in one-party states. These inequalities have nurtured our moderate two-party system.

Preceding chapters discuss the electoral system's discrimination against third parties. Since it gives the second major party (the out party) the monopoly of opposition, it reinforces the nominations by party conventions and requires the parties to seek broad national support. In addition, the state unit system discriminates against ideological and extremist voters and parties and is a safeguard against factionalism. The geographic-dispersion requirement forced on the national parties has undercut any tendencies to organize on class, economic, or ideological lines. The fact that minority voters within each state cannot combine their votes across state lines may not be too large a price to pay for nonideological parties. Those who focus on the integrity of each individual vote in depicting the popular will disregard the political necessity of constructing that will. The popular will does not exist as a completely formed yet unsurveyed territory to which we need only send technicians equipped with accurate measuring devices. Rather, there are many wills, many separate interests (some moderate, some immoderate) clustered here and there, which must be molded into a majority. At present this service is performed for our polity by the political parties. The object is to create political majorities, not arithmetical majorities. Ours is a pluralistic nation with a wide variety of interests and traditions, ethnic and religious, and this pluralism is one of the conditions of our moderate two parties. But it may not be the sufficient condition, for it is conceivable that the national parties could form along class or strict ideological lines. Perhaps one reason they have not is that the parties need wide geographic support. "The pluralism of social interests combined with a party's need for wide geographic support," writes Allan Sindler, "coerces both major parties into adopting similar, moderate policies." He concludes that it is in the interest of each party to attract "something like the same cross-section of the population, rather than exclusive segments."[47]

Because elections under the unit rule are often decided in the pivotal or partisanly doubtful states, each party is forced to make a broad appeal for votes. It dare not rely

47. Allan Sindler, *Political Parties in the United States* (New York, 1966), p. 81.

on its own hard core of followers. In addition, ideological groups are discriminated against by the unit rule, which prevents an effective merger of their national voting power. A segregationist party cannot effectively combine votes across state lines, nor can a black separatist party. It is not in the interest of either major party totally to ignore some major interest groups or abandon them to the opposition. In the 1968 election the distribution of the black vote between the major parties aroused concern in all quarters. Nixon had the support of only 740,000 blacks, but Humphrey of 6,500,000. It is not politically healthy for the Democrats to become or to be thought of as the "party dominated by Northern labor unions, big city minority blocs, and ideologues who control the new campus proletariat."[48] Nor is it healthy for the blacks to be so completely identified with one party, for when that party is out of power the appearance of isolation may result in embitterment. Nor is it healthy for the Republicans when they must govern. It is in the national interest that the winning party and candidate be at least acceptable to all groups.

No major party can afford to take an extreme stand on any issue, because it must build majorities and distribute its strength in a large number of separate geographical units. Theodore H. White reports that while efforts were made by both major parties to undercut the Wallace appeal in 1968, "to compete with Wallace on any civilized level was impossible—thus, states like Alabama, Mississippi and Louisiana and several others were scratched as targets."[49]

48. White, *Making of the President, 1968*, p. 401.
49. *Ibid.*, p. 331.

Though some of the charges of voter inequality have more substance than others, the answer to all of them is that they do not take into account the political and governmental structure as a whole. Currently the Presidency tends to overrepresent the large urban states and key minority groups within those states, and it overrepresents competitive states and underrepresents the small rural, one-party states. The Congress tends to do the opposite. The President does not hold all the reins of power in our polity. The power system is federal, decentralized, Madisonian, and, to a degree usually unrecognized, approaches a system of "unanimous" consent. The nation has sought and largely achieved a system that reflects the views and interests of broad cross sections of the polity. Negotiation, compromise, and consultation with the particular interests most fundamentally affected have been characteristic of our power struture. Almost every major interest in the country has access to the power structure. Some interests have looked primarily to the courts, some to the states, some to the independent agencies, some to the Congress, some to the Presidency.

Despite the failure of Calhoun's theory of nullification, his basic principle, "the principle which Calhoun called—rather obscurely—the rule of the concurrent majority, has become the organizing principle of American politics."[50] Nowhere is the evidence for this proposition more clearly found than in the Congress. Although the Congress is formally organized on geographic lines, because of religious,

50. Peter F. Drucker, "A Key to Calhoun's Pluralism," *Review of Politics* 10 (1948), 413.

ethnic, and occupational clustering, the division is not merely geographic. James Burnham concludes that the Congress represents concurrent majorities:

The Congressman from New Mexico is also Congressman of the Mexican-Spanish stock; the member from Boston, of the urban Irish, as the New Yorker of the urban Jews. The gentleman from Montana, Nevada and Colorado can speak for the mining industry. Through the Cleveland or Pittsburgh or Gary member, Congress hears the voice of the steel mills. The auto workers can send their ambassadors from Detroit or Flint.[51]

Calhoun was not breaking new ground when he proposed the concept of the concurrent majority. Strands of this theory can be traced back to Madison, *The Federalist Papers* 10 and 51, and also to Rousseau's *Social Contract*.[52] Neal Peirce admits that "the theory is still attractive and valid in many ways." But he argues that it is "inapplicable to the election of a single individual—the President of the United States."[53] The Presidency, however, cannot be abstracted from the system simply because the President is a single individual. He is the particular individual in whom one of the tripartite powers, the executive power, is lodged. He is the individual who may, among a host of other things, exercise the veto, make appointments, and compel obedience to the

51. *Congress and the American Tradition* (Chicago, 1959), pp. 327–328.

52. Robert Dahl, *A Preface to Democratic Theory* (Chicago, 1956); George Kateb, "The Majority Principle: Calhoun and His Antecedents," *Political Science Quarterly* 84 (1969), 583.

53. Peirce, *People's President*, p. 255.

laws. The Presidency is an integral part of the system of checks and balances. Any fundamental change in the Presidency is a fundamental change in the entire system.

Our essentially Madisonian regime seeks two often conflicting goals: majority rule and political liberty. Robert Dahl claims that Madisonian Democracy attempts to "bring off a compromise between the power of majorities and the power of minorities, between the political equality of all adult citizens on the one side, and the desire to limit their sovereignty on the other."[54] The fear of majority tyranny was one of the most fundamental influences on the Founders. The idea of one man, one equally weighted vote cannot be laid at their door, as the Constitution itself proclaims.

The very idea of a written constitution, a fundamental law, a law superior to the will of ordinary majorities is an offense to populistic democracy. It is true that this fundamental law can be altered, but only by extraordinary federal majorities. And a strong case can be made that at least one section, that giving each state equal representation in the Senate as long as it wills, cannot be altered even by the amendment procedure.[55] The rule of one man, one equally weighted vote does not apply to the amendment process, for each state has one vote, and the votes of three-fourths of the states are necessary for ratification. This means that the votes in one-fourth of the states plus one "weigh" more

54. *Preface to Democratic Theory*, p. 4.
55. Edward S. Corwin, *The Constitution and What It Means Today* (New York, 1964), p. 177.

than the votes in three-fourths minus one. It does not matter whether the one-fourth plus one is composed of the least populous states in the union or if those states reject the amendment by the narrowest possible margin.

The list of constitutional limitations on the majority is a long one, including the Supreme Court, the Senate, the guarantee of at least one congressman to each state, and the extraordinary majorities required for the Senate to convict those impeached by the House, for Congress to expel one of its members, and for Congress to override a presidential veto. In addition, the Constitution places certain limitations on even a unanimous Congress, restrictions designed to protect individuals and minorities, such as the provisions respecting the writ of habeas corpus, the bill of attainder, and ex post facto laws. Other restrictions are placed directly on the states.

These are but some of the formal restrictions. Within the Congress institutional procedures and norms are not always in strict accord with majority rule. The Senate filibuster, the seniority rule, the committee system all are deviations from the principle of political equality. Many of the institutional procedures and norms are designed to reward longevity and to encourage expertise, not to give political equality. Moreover, congressmen, senators, and the President are elected in different ways for different terms. The reason underlying this complex mode of filling our national elective offices was to prevent temporary majorities from controlling the whole government.

The Founders desired to institute a popular government and, above all, a free government. To this end they set a multitude of restrictions upon the formation and influence of all-national majorities—restrictions against factionalism and dominant interests adverse to the rights of individuals. The direct election of the President would be the first all-national election in our history. There is no precedent for it; not even the Constitution was adopted by a direct all-national vote.

This constitutional framework has allowed the development of concurrent majorities, and, according to George Kateb, the true significance of concurrent majorities in America is that they offend the majoritarian principle of equal weight to all votes.[56] This system has not been short on critics. The concurrent majority has many weaknesses: it cannot resolve deep principled divisions in a society; it often is dilatory and sluggish; it cannot claim to speak clearly and directly for the national interest; and it is not logically consistent. On the positive side, concurrent majorities mean stability, accommodation, and moderation.

This constitutional system, this power structure may not be logically consistent, but it is ours. To say it is ours is not to say it is the best; however, it may be the best possible, the best under the conditions and accidents of history, of population, of territory. We are now being asked to tamper with part of this system in the name of political equality. Senator John Kennedy put the case in its now classic form: "When all these factors are considered, it is not the unit vote for the Presidency we are talking about, but a whole solar system of governmental power. If it is proposed to

56. "The Majority Principle," p. 583.

change the balance of power of one of the elements of the solar system, it is necessary to consider all the others."[57]

In disagreeing with the reformers on this issue, defenders of the electoral-vote system do not deny that political equality is a legitimate goal under the Constitution; they do deny that it is the only goal. As Tocqueville brilliantly foresaw, political equality is quite compatible with tyranny: men who make equality their idol will "prefer equality in slavery to inequality with freedom."[58]

The Founders, fearing the rise of dominant interests adverse to the rights of others, established a system of separated powers, of checks and balances, as a "security against the gradual concentration of the several powers in the same departments."[59] The Founders believed the greatest danger of encroachment would arise in the strong legislature and would be directed against the weak executive. Their anticipation of a strong legislature and a weak executive has not been fulfilled with the passage of time. The ascendance and expansion of the power of the Presidency have been among the most profound and notable developments in the history of the republic. They have been analyzed, dissected, criticized, and praised by a host of scholars. The polity has a strong, innovative, energetic Presidency which is the focal point of public attention. The mode of election of the Presi-

57. *Congressional Record*, Vol. 102, Pt. 4, 84th Cong., 2d sess. (1956), p. 5150.

58. Alexis de Tocqueville, *Democracy in America*, ed. Richard D. Heffner (New York, 1956), p. 55.

59. *The Federalist Papers*, ed. Clinton Rossiter (New York, 1961), No. 51, p. 321.

dent has a great bearing on the nature of the office and on the kind of men who are chosen to fill that office. The direct election of our national executive, unprecedented in our history, would be a fundamental change in our system. The President speaks for the nation as no one in the Congress can. But the voice of the President as the voice of the people is somewhat softened by his indirect election in fifty-one separate constituencies. The direct election could clarify that voice, could strengthen an already strong presidential office. Congress is presently overshadowed by the gigantic stature of the Presidency. We may pause and consider whether we wish to strengthen the Presidency further.

On a higher level, we must consider whether we have outgrown the dangers of factionalism, whether we wish to change the balance in a system designed to reflect the interests of broad cross sections of the country. Would the election of the President by a direct vote of the nation as a whole make him more responsive to the will of the people? That depends on what we understand the will of the people to be. A direct election with one man, one equally weighted vote aims at the will of the numerical majority. Let us not forget, however, that the majority is only a part of the people. Carl Becker reminds us that "the will of the people is at best an intangible thing, and it is a delusion to suppose that it can be determined in all circumstances by majority vote."[60]

60. "The Will of the People," *Yale Review* 34 (March 1945), p. 391.

5 The Faithless Elector

> I have found that holding the office of elector is a very
> responsible position, and it should not be taken lightly as
> is the case today. It demands time-consuming study, for-
> titude, total allegiance to our country, and a love of all
> that we hold dear in our American way of life. I am
> appealing to your good judgment and your own love of
> country, with the hope that you will seriously consider
> the possibility of restoring presidential electors to the
> positions which they were originally intended to hold.
>
> Dr. Lloyd W. Bailey[1]

Dr. Lloyd W. Bailey, a Republican elector from North
Carolina, cast his ballot in the electoral college in 1968 for
George Wallace. Dr. Bailey, who had attended a district
convention of the Republican party of North Carolina in
February 1968, was nominated as a Republican elector
months before the party's presidential candidate was chosen
in its national convention. Dr. Bailey took no formal pledge
and reports that there was no discussion of party loyalty or
of commitment to any particular candidate. So lightly is the
position of elector taken that Dr. Bailey forgot he was an

1. Statement to U.S. Senate, Committee on the Judiciary, Subcommittee on Constitutional Amendments; in *Hearings, Electing
the President*, 91st Cong., 1st sess., 1969, p. 40 (cited hereafter as
1969 Senate *Hearings*).

elector until reminded by a party official a few weeks before the election.[2] According to his own account, Dr. Bailey did not give much more thought to his position until President-elect Richard Nixon began to make appointments two weeks before the meeting of the electoral college. Dr. Bailey referred specifically to the appointments of Robert D. Murphy, Henry A. Kissinger, Paul W. McCracken, and Daniel Moynihan. These appointments, Nixon's policy statements, and his request that Chief Justice Earl Warren remain on the Court until June 1969 crystallized Dr. Bailey's decision to cast his electoral-college ballot for Wallace: "The primary reason for my vote was to protest the fact that President-elect Nixon was not going to change the course of our government in spite of the overwhelming vote in the general election against the policies of the Johnson administration."[3]

His decision was reinforced by Wallace's victory in his congressional district.[4] Wallace polled 46.1 percent of the vote in the Second Congressional District of North Carolina. Hubert Humphrey came in second, with 31.6 percent, and Nixon third, with 22.3 percent. Dr. Bailey's reliance on the Wallace plurality in his district was, at the very least, ill-advised, for although the North Carolina electors are initially nominated from each congressional district, their nominations are confirmed in a state party convention and they are elected in a statewide contest. Their names are not on the ballot, and only those of the candidates for President

2. *Ibid.*, p. 37.
3. *Ibid.*, pp. 37–38.
4. *Ibid.*, p. 50.

and Vice-President are.[5] Dr. Bailey was not chosen as an elector from the Second Congressional District of North Carolina but as an elector for the entire state. His claim that "there would have been more people in my district who would not have been represented had I done otherwise" is completely refuted by the fact that the 627,192 North Carolinians who voted for Nixon in 1968 were deprived of one-thirteenth of their lawful electoral votes.[6] In fact, if the electors had been chosen by districts, Dr. Bailey, as the Republican elector, would not have been chosen. But the doctor's reference to the Wallace district victory was more of an afterthought, for in the interval between the general election and the meeting of the college, he changed his mind. Until President-elect Nixon indicated the direction of his administration, Dr. Bailey "just assumed automatically that [he] would go up with the rest and just vote as they did because it was the thing to do."[7]

Dr. Bailey's action provoked a storm of protest; he was castigated editorially as the "defector elector," and by an overwhelming majority of congressmen in a heated constitutional debate over the power of the Congress to vacate his vote. In an exchange with Senator Thurmond during a Senate hearing, Dr. Bailey admitted that his vote was primarily a protest vote:

5. Francis Valeo, Richard C. Hupman, and Robert Tienken, *Nomination and Election of the President and Vice President of the United States: Including the Manner of Selecting Delegates to National Political Conventions* (Washington, 1968), p. 220.

6. 1969 Senate *Hearings*, p. 55.

7. *Ibid.*, p. 58.

Senator Thurmond. As I understand, you ran on the Nixon ticket, and expected to vote for Mr. Nixon, but after the election because of certain positions that you didn't feel were wise for the country, you felt it your obligation.

Dr. Bailey. Yes, Sir.

Senator Thurmond. To vote for Mr. Wallace?

Dr. Bailey. Right.

Senator Thurmond. Although you wouldn't have voted for Mr. Wallace if there had been danger of it going to the House because Mr. Humphrey might have been elected?

Dr. Bailey. That is right.[8]

Because North Carolina has no law expressly binding an elector to vote for the winner of the statewide popular vote, and because no challenge was made to this elector's action in North Carolina, the next scenes in this untimely revival of the unfaithful elector were played in the Senate and the House.

Unquestionably, an elector's decision to exercise his discretion to override the expectations of the voters in his state is an act of betrayal and a violation of a moral obligation. Lucius Wilmerding is probably correct when he says, "There has never been a single occasion and I doubt if there ever is one when the eccentricities of the electors have changed the result of an election."[9] The faithlessness of even a single elector, however, thwarts the will and expectations of the voters in his state. More important, as long as the nation continues the present electoral-college system, it accepts the risk that in a close election errant electors could

8. *Ibid.*, p. 43.
9. *The Electoral College* (New Brunswick, N.J., 1958), p. 205.

hold the balance of power and that the result of the contest could turn on their votes.

Although the risk is extremely remote, the dissatisfaction with human electors and the moral outrage aroused by faithless electors have been a force behind the automatic reform plan, which would retain the electoral-count system, abolish the office of elector, and automatically award each state's electoral votes to the candidate with a plurality in the state. The idea is an old one; it was first proposed by Senator Thomas Hart Benton in 1823. Jefferson is credited with having suggested it in a letter to Gallatin in 1801.[10] Acceptance of the automatic plan, as Sayre and Parris point out, would effect a minimal change; they therefore suggest that "the major question that remains about the automatic plan is whether the small amount of change it entails justifies the effort required to pass a constitutional amendment."[11] A constitutional amendment should be a last resort to remedy a serious and substantive problem. We should not change the Constitution lightly or without having tried extraconstitutional approaches.

Albert Rosenthal indicates three ways to eliminate faithless electors: "by the courts under existing law, by statute, or by constitutional amendment."[12] The first alternative, action by the courts under existing law, is a doubtful

10. Cited in Wilmerding, *Electoral College*, p. 169.

11. Wallace S. Sayre and Judith H. Parris, *Voting for President: The Electoral College and the American Political System* (Washington, 1972), p. 101.

12. "The Constitution, Congress and Presidential Elections," *Michigan Law Review* 67 (1968–1969), 17.

possibility and could not provide an entirely satisfactory solution.[13] Opinion is divided on the untrammeled freedom of the electors under the Constitution. In *Ray* v. *Blair,* the majority of the justices did not reach the issue of whether a state may compel a duly chosen elector to vote for the winner in his state. However, in the view of the two dissenting justices, Robert H. Jackson and William O. Douglas, the states cannot tamper with the constitutional discretion of the electors.[14] Dicta in several state decisions are in accord with the two.[15] On the other hand, constitutional discretion has almost universally been abandoned by electors for over 150 years. In addition, a number of state laws require pledges from candidates for the office of elector, and several states, in statutory instructions, direct the electors to honor their commitments.

Even if the electors can be bound, if the state laws that attempt to bind them are constitutional, enforceability poses a problem. If an elector announced his intention to violate his pledge prior to the meeting of the college, there would be at least two possible remedies open to the courts, a mandamus or an injunction. Whether a court could issue a mandamus is in itself questionable; according to Rosenthal, "there may be some doubt as to the propriety of mandamus where the time for the official act has not yet arrived."[16] If

13. For a full treatment see Rosenthal, "The Constitution."

14. *Ray* v. *Blair,* 343 U.S. 214 (1952).

15. *Opinion of the Justices,* No. 87, 250 Ala. 399, 400, 34 S. 2d 589, 600 (1948); *State ex rel. Beck* v. *Hummel,* 150 Ohio St. 127, 146, 80 N.E. 2d 899, 908 (1948); *Briendenthal* v. *Edwards,* 57 Kans. 332, 337, 460, 469, 470 (1896).

16. "The Constitution," p. 25.

an elector ignored the mandamus and voted according to his whim, a state might punish him, but could it change his already cast vote? If a court enjoined an elector from voting for anyone but the candidate to whom he was pledged, he could abstain from voting at all and thus disfranchise a great number of voters. And if the potential defector kept his own counsel, made no previous announcement, and simply voted according to his own light on the appointed day, what recourse would the courts have? Does the power of the state to appoint electors extend to recasting an already cast vote? This question has not been resolved and would certainly require a test before the Supreme Court.

Moreover, there is doubt that the question is justiciable. The Supreme Court might decide that it was not, because under Article II, Section 1, the Congress has the power to count the electoral votes. Under *Baker* v. *Carr* the Court could find that the power of Congress to count the votes bars judicial action, for "it is the relationship between the judiciary and the co-ordinate branches of the government which gives rise to the political question."[17]

The power of the Congress to count the votes has been the subject of much controversy in our history, largely because of a serious error in the drafting of the original constitutional directions, which was continued in the Twelfth Amendment: "The President of the Senate shall, in the Presence of the Senate and the House of Representatives, open all the Certificates, and the Votes shall then be counted."[18] A question arose as to who had the constitu-

17. *Baker* v. *Carr*, 369 U.S. 186 (1962).
18. U.S. Constitution, Art. II, Sec. 1.

tional power to count the votes. With the passage of time this question has been resolved in favor of the Congress as a whole and against the President of the Senate. L. Kinvin Wroth traces the historical development of the congressional power over the electoral-vote count from its inception through the passage of the Electoral Count Act of 1887, the statutory law that controls the congressional count. He finds many potential problems under that act; in addition, he makes an interesting case for lodging exclusive jurisdiction of contests in the federal courts.[19] Since his article was written, the Congress has, for the first time since the Electoral Count Act was passed, entertained an objection to the counting of an electoral vote and engaged in a full-dress debate under the provisions of the law. This debate revealed serious drawbacks to Rosenthal's second proposal that faithless electors be eliminated by an act of Congress.

The Congress of the United States was meeting in joint session on January 6, 1969, to fulfill its constitutional duty of counting the electoral votes. Just after the teller had read the certificate of the vote from North Carolina, a congressman from Michigan, James G. O'Hara, rose to object to the counting of the vote of North Carolina as read. In compliance with the law, O'Hara submitted a written objection signed by himself and Senator Edmund Muskie of Maine, who were joined by thirty-seven members of the House and six members of the Senate. Pursuant to the law, the two bodies separated to determine their respective positions.

19. L. Kinvin Wroth, "Election Contests and the Electoral Vote," *Dickinson Law Review* 65 (1961), 321.

The debate that followed sorely tried the members' dedication to a government of laws and not of men.

The issue was whether the voters of North Carolina had a right to have their votes faithfully reflected in the electoral count, and if they had a right did they have a remedy and a recourse against a faithless elector who substituted his will for theirs. The Muskie-O'Hara complaint was based on the statute enacted in 1887 and currently incorporated in the United States Code, Title 3, Section 15, which stipulates that "no electoral vote or votes from any state which shall have been regularly given by electors whose appointment has been lawfully certified . . . but from which but one return has been received shall be rejected, but the two Houses concurrently may reject the vote or votes when they agree that such vote or votes have not been so certified."

The meaning of "regularly given" was at the heart of the question, and the statute did not define it. Among the many possible irregularities are votes cast on an improper day, votes for an ineligible candidate (one not thirty-five years old or a natural-born citizen), votes cast by a "state" not lawfully in the Union on the day appointed for casting the votes, and dual returns. But whether a vote cast in a state conceded to be in the Union, on the proper day, for an eligible candidate, and certified and unchallenged by the proper state authorities could be vacated for any reason except a formal or procedural irregularity was questionable.

Prior to 1961, when Hawaii presented the Congress with dual returns, Congress had not been called upon to interpret the statute. On that occasion, the outcome of the election was not affected, and the joint session counted the votes of the Democratic electors. This situation must be distinguished from that in 1969, because the former clearly fell under the statutory section on double returns. The weight of precedent applicable to single returns was not on the side of Muskie and O'Hara. In the years between the founding and 1969, 16,510 electors had been chosen, and only 6, in all those years, had clearly "miscast" their ballots. In every case, even when the betrayal was roundly deplored, the ballots were counted as cast.

Several of these cases occurred after the passage of the Electoral Count Act in 1887. In 1948, a Tennessee elector, Preston Parks, who ran on two slates, one committed to Truman and one to Thurmond, voted for Thurmond even though the Truman ticket carried the state. In 1956, an Alabama elector, W. F. Turner, voted for Judge Walter E. Jones instead of for Adlai Stevenson. In 1960, an Oklahoma elector cast his vote for Harry Flood Byrd instead of for Nixon, who carried his state.

A further precedent is provided by the election of 1872. Horace Greeley, the Democratic candidate, won the popular vote in six states. Shortly after the election, and before the meeting of the electoral college, he died. Most of Greeley's sixty-six electors scattered their votes among a number of other men. Thomas Hendricks received forty-two; Benjamin Brown, eighteen; Charles Jenkins, two; and David Davis, one. These votes were all officially accepted and counted by the Congress. Three Georgia electors, however, persisted in voting for Greeley, but the Congress refused to count their votes, on the ground that they were not cast for a person. In 1912, the defeated Republican vice-presidential candidate, James Sherman, who ran on the ticket with Taft, died before the electoral college met. The eight electors the two had won cast their vice-presidential votes for Nicholas Murray Butler, to ensure their votes' being counted. Congressman McCulloch of Ohio suggested that Congress could not "have it both ways—electors who are bound if the candidates live and electors who are independent if the candidates die."[20]

Thus, despite a century and a half of constitutional usage, which, it is argued, has modified the original independence of the electors, the Congress in the past has read the language of the Constitution ("The electors shall . . . vote by ballot for President and Vice President") to mean the electors are free and independent in their act of voting.

Senator Muskie conceded that the language of the Constitution clearly contemplates free electors, but he nevertheless argued that since, according to the Supreme Court ruling in *Ray* v. *Blair*, an elector can be bound by a pledge to his party under a state statute, an elector may therefore bind himself, "especially as in North Carolina, where his name does not appear on the ballot."[21] He argued further that, in accepting his party's nomination for the office of elector, Dr. Bailey did so bind himself. According to Senator Muskie's interpretation of the 1887 statute, the certification of the electors relates only to their election, and the congressional authority to determine whether or not the

20. *Congressional Record*, Vol. 115, Pt. 1, 91st Cong., 1st sess. (1969), p. 148.
21. *Ibid.*, p. 205.

votes are "regularly given" is the authority to determine whether an elector is bound, either by his state or by his own act.

Senator Sam Ervin of North Carolina, in rebuttal, contended that his state's law providing that "a vote for the candidates named on the ballot shall be a vote for the elector of the party by which those candidates were nominated" cannot be construed as an attempt to bind the electors.[22] The senator from North Carolina informed Muskie that the intention of the statute was to simplify the ballot and to avoid confusion. And Senator Ervin, who enjoys the reputation of being a constitutional scholar, noted that in *Ray* v. *Blair*, the Supreme Court upheld an Alabama statute empowering a political party to require a pledge to support the party's nominees from anyone who wished to run as a presidential elector, and to exclude him if he refused to take such a pledge. The Supreme Court did not go further. It did not say that a state can control the vote of an elector, nor did it hold that Congress has a right to control the vote of an elector. The only obligation that Dr. Bailey had assumed was an ethical one, and according to Senator Ervin, the objection to Dr. Bailey's vote was an attempt to convert this ethical obligation into a legal one.

Despite the Muskie-O'Hara interpretation, a strong case can be made that the original intention of the Electoral Act was to require all future contests to be resolved in the state or states where they developed.[23] This act was provoked by the Hayes-Tilden election and by the findings of the re-

22. General Statutes, North Carolina, Secs. 163, 209.
23. Wroth, "Election Contests," p. 321.

sulting congressional Electoral Commission. Instead of giving Congress the power to control the vote of an elector, the intention of the statute seems to be the opposite: to prevent Congress from vacating any vote that is certified by a state and that is procedurally and formally regular; and to make the state's determination conclusive whenever it sends only a single certificate properly signed by the governor under the state's seal. According to the "Report of the House Select Committee on the Election of the President," given in 1886, the statute was designed to bind the Congress to accept the determination of contests by the authorities provided by a state. "Congress having provided by this bill that State tribunals may determine what votes are legal coming from that State, and that the two Houses shall be bound by this determination, it will be that State's own fault if the matter is left in doubt."[24] In his study of election contests, L. Kinvin Wroth concludes that "the contest provisions of the Electoral Count Act were intended to provide a balance of the state interest in the process of appointment and the federal interest in reaching a result free of fraud or unfairness in time to inaugurate the winning candidate."[25]

In 1969, North Carolina made no complaint. It did not send in dual returns, nor did it appeal to the Congress for redress. On the contrary, the chairman of the State Board of Elections issued a statement condemning the attempt by the Congress to usurp the state's authority.

It is simply beyond reasonable comprehension that the Fed-

24. H.R. Report 1638, 49th Cong., 2d sess., 18 *Congressional Record*, 30 (1886).

25. "Election Contests," p. 344.

eral Congress or any segment thereof would presume to alter the electoral vote from North Carolina or any other state. There is no constitutional authority for such action nor is there any basis in law for the Congress to disrupt this due process.[26]

Senator Muskie did find a legal precedent to support his argument, in *Thomas* v. *Cohen*.[27] In this New York case a challenge was made to the constitutionality of the practice of putting only the names of the presidential candidates on the ballot. In upholding the state's practice, the court said:

The electors are expected to choose the nominee of the party they represent, and no one else. So sacred and compelling is that obligation upon them, so long has its observance been recognized by faithful performance, so unexpected and destructive of order in our land would be its violation, that the trust that was originally conferred upon the electors by the people, to express their will by the selections they make, has, over these many years, ripened into a bounden duty—as binding upon them as if it were written into the organic law.[28]

The long-standing and almost universal custom of electors as mere recorders does not mean that the states have expressly bound the electors. And the idea that the Constitution can be diametrically altered by a practice inconsistent with its language or simply by the passage of time is not one that many will enthusiastically endorse. Justice Jackson, in *Ray* v. *Blair*, expresses his view: "But I do not think powers

26. Quoted in *Congressional Record*, Vol. 115, Pt. 1, 91st Cong., 1st sess. (1969), p. 150.

27. *Thomas* v. *Cohen*, 146 Misc. 836, 841–844, 262 N.Y.S. 320, 326 (Sup. Ct., 1933).

28. *Ibid.*, pp. 841–842.

or discretions granted to federal officials by the federal Constitution can be forfeited by the Court for disuse. A political practice which has its origin in custom must rely on custom for its sanctions."[29]

Thomas v. *Cohen* is the only case that suggests that an elector may be compelled to cast his vote as his party directs. Two other cases seem to be premised on the notion that an elector has a legal, as opposed to a moral, obligation to support his party's nominees.[30] But neither in these two cases nor in any other did a court go so far as to say, as it did in *Thomas* v. *Cohen*, that there is any remedy for an elector's failure to vote as his party directs. In *Thomas*, the court suggested a mandamus could be issued to compel an elector.

In 1912 the Nebraska Supreme Court granted a mandamus to compel the Secretary of State to print on the ballot the names of persons other than the six Roosevelt men originally nominated by the Republican party.[31] Roosevelt had won the Nebraska Republican preference primary, but Taft was nominated by the national party convention. The six Roosevelt men were subsequently chosen as the nominees for electors of the Nebraska Progressive party and refused to withdraw from the Republican slate. The Court decided that, in accepting the latter nomination, these men had vacated their places as Republican electors. In this case

29. *Ray* v. *Blair*, 233.

30. *State ex rel. Nebraska Republican State Cent. Comm.* v. *Wait*, 92 Neb. 313, 325, 138 N.W. 159, 163 (1912); *Johnson* v. *Coyne*, 47 S.D. 138, 142, 196 N.W. 492, 493 (1923).

31. *Nebraska Republican Cent. Comm.* v. *Wait.*

the mandamus was directed to the Secretary of State prior to the election. It was not directed to duly elected presidential electors.

Some senators, including Edward Brooke of Massachusetts, took the position that if a state has actually bound its electors, the Congress can properly act, but "unless the state chooses to bind its electors the Congress cannot do so after the fact."[32] Senator Brooke found that North Carolina had not actually bound its electors, and therefore decided that Dr. Bailey's vote should stand. Several objections can be raised against Senator Brooke's position. It is not yet certain that the states can, in fact, bind electors; the United States Supreme Court has not ruled on this matter. And if they can, it is not clear whether there is a remedy for violation. An Alabama law ordering electors to cast their ballots for the nominee of their party was declared unconstitutional by the Alabama Supreme Court prior to the 1948 election.[33] In a petition the United States Supreme Court was asked to enjoin the Alabama electors from voting for candidates other than their party's nominees, but the Court refused to entertain the suit.[34] The justices of the Supreme Court of Alabama, in an advisory opinion to the governor, concluded:

When the legislature has provided for the appointment of electors its powers and functions have ended. If and when it attempts to go further and dictate to the electors the choice

32. *Congressional Record*, Vol. 115, Pt. 1, 91st Cong., 1st sess. (1969), p. 213.
33. *Opinion of the Justices.*
34. *Folsom* v. *Albritton*, 335 U.S. 882 (1948).

which they must make for president and vice president, it has invaded the field set apart to the electors by the Constitution of the United States and such an action cannot stand.[35]

In a 1948 Ohio case, *State* ex rel. *Beck* v. *Hummel,* the state court stated that "according to the federal Constitution a presidential elector may vote for any person he pleases for President or Vice President provided that person be a natural born citizen of the United States, shall have attained the age of 35 years and been 14 years a resident within the United States."[36] This decision was in keeping with an early Kansas case decided in 1896 wherein the court stated that electors are under no legal obligation to support any person named by a political party and that no court can interfere with their performance of their duties.[37]

Opinion is divided as to whether electors can be bound. Several commentators have made a good case for the states' power to bind them,[38] and several states have attempted to do so. In 1968 four states and the District of Columbia required an oath or a pledge from nominees for the office of elector. Failure to vote for their party's candidates in Florida may result in liability for a felony. In New Mexico and Oklahoma electors who violate their instructions are guilty of a misdemeanor; in the latter, the fine may be as

35. *Opinion of the Justices,* 401.
36. *Beck* v. *Hummel,* 146.
37. *Briendenthal* v. *Edwards,* 332.
38. "State Power to Bind Presidential Electors," *Columbia Law Review* 65 (1965), 696–709; James C. Kirby, Jr., "Limitations on the Power of State Legislatures over Presidential Elections," *Law and Contemporary Problems* 27 (1962), 495–509; Rosenthal, "The Constitution, Congress and Presidential Elections," pp. 1–38.

much as one thousand dollars. Nine states expressly instruct their electors to cast their votes for the candidates of their party or for the plurality winner in the state. A total of fifteen states and the District of Columbia have, by requiring an oath or pledge or by specific statutory instruction, attempted to bind the electors. Of the remaining states, twenty-four use the short ballot, without the electors' names. In these states, it may be argued, there is an implied instruction to the electors; or it may be argued, as Senator Ervin did, that the mere adoption of the short ballot carries no such implication. The fact that, in 1968, thirty-five states used the short ballot and that, of these, at least eleven believed it additionally necessary to require a pledge, threaten a penalty, or specifically instruct the electors casts doubt on the theory that the short ballot in itself binds the electors.[39]

Even if Senator Brooke is correct in assuming that the state legislatures may bind the electors, and even if Congress can provide a remedy for violation of a pledge, it can only act when the states have, in fact, bound the electors. In only fifteen states and the District of Columbia could it have been said that they had clearly and unequivocally attempted to bind the electors. Furthermore, even if it is assumed that the states have the right to bind the electors, a right that arises from their constitutional power to appoint electors, there may be no remedy for a miscast vote. There are penalties for violation, but no state has a provision for recasting a miscast vote. If the Congress takes upon itself the duty of

39. The figures are from Valeo, Hupman, and Tienken, *Nomination and Election.* See also Sayre and Parris, *Voting for President,* p. 41.

enforcing pledges, its recourse may be, as Muskie and O'Hara proposed, to vacate the vote of a faithless elector. This remedy was highly unsatisfactory to many members, because it would have reduced North Carolina's constitutional allotment of electoral votes. Senator Ralph Yarborough stated that "to vote to deny North Carolina one of her electoral votes is to attempt to amend the Constitution of the United States by act of the Congress alone."[40]

The original goal of the Muskie-O'Hara complaint was not only to vacate the Bailey vote, but also to declare that the vote be cast for Nixon and Agnew. The leaders of the movement against the faithless elector decided, on the advice of the parliamentarians of both houses, to limit their request to vacating the vote, because they feared if both requests were made the House and the Senate could take different actions. If the House, for example, voted to vacate the vote but not to recast it, and the Senate voted to do both, the challenge would not be sustained, according to the provisions of the Electoral Count Act.

Despite the limitation on the formal objection, some congressmen wished to vacate the vote and to recast it for Nixon. Among them was the chairman of the House Committee on the Judiciary, Emanuel Celler, who thought that because the Congress has the right to count the votes, "it can be understood that [Congress] can cast the vote for Mr. Nixon."[41] Celler's understanding to the contrary, it may

40. *Congressional Record,* Vol. 115, Pt. 1, 91st Cong., 1st sess. (1969), p. 217.
41. *Ibid.,* p. 149.

be argued that there is a difference between counting a vote and casting a vote. If the power of the Congress to count the votes is interpreted as the power to recast the votes, the cure may turn out to be worse than the disease. Dr. Bailey's vote was cast in the regular manner and lawfully certified. To contend that it was irregularly given is to declare that the fact of his vote was the irregularity. If the Congress can vacate and recast electoral votes, it may be argued that Congress can expropriate the power to elect the President.

Since every member of Congress is constitutionally barred from serving as a presidential elector, can the aggregate constitutionally perform a function denied to the individual? In addition, the recast vote would not have been cast on the proper day; according to the Constitution all electoral votes must be cast on the same day. Gerald R. Ford, who admitted that sustaining the Muskie-O'Hara challenge would set a bad precedent, nevertheless decided he would support the challenge and count the votes of the "people of North Carolina." But North Carolina sent only one certificate. If the Congress can count a vote that has not been certified by a state, is the Congress usurping the power of the states to appoint presidential electors?

Despite the universal sympathy of the Congress, the majority in both Houses interpreted the constitutional power of the Congress to count the vote as a ministerial, quasi-judicial function. In the words of Senator Carl Curtis: "We are not called upon to decide how we think the vote ought to be counted. We are not called upon to decide what we think ought to be the law. We are called upon to count the votes according to the law as it exists today and as it existed during the recent election."[42] The attempt to vacate Dr. Bailey's vote in the joint session held on January 6, 1969, failed, thereby establishing one more precedent against this alternative. The Congress, by a vote of 169 to 229 in the House, and of 33 to 58 in the Senate, interpreted its constitutional duty as the power "to count electoral votes, not to cast them, nor to ignore them, nor to recast them."[43]

There are too many drawbacks to a congressional solution to the problem of the faithless elector. The Muskie-O'Hara remedy was interpreted by some members, particularly those from North Carolina, as an offense to state control over the process of appointment of presidential electors. A congressional solution, particularly one which not only vacates but also recasts electoral votes deemed irregular for nonprocedural reasons, comes dangerously close to arrogating the power to elect the President to the Congress. Since the rules for the congressional count are in statutory law, any existing law could be overturned to favor one candidate over another, because the new Congress meets on January 3, three days prior to the joint session which counts the electoral votes.

A congressional solution might not end the controversy, for an elector whose vote was vacated might bring suit to have it counted as cast. Although it is inconceivable that any court would issue a mandamus to an officer of the Congress and although a court could refuse to hear the case as involving a political question, there remains the possibility

42. *Ibid.*, p. 219.
43. Statement of Congressman Nick Galifianakis, *Ibid.*, p. 162.

of the *Marbury* v. *Madison* situation, with the court stating the elector had a right but not a remedy. Or worse, the court might rule against the elector and uphold the right of Congress to recast a procedurally regular electoral vote. Finally, a congressional solution would not eliminate the basic problem of allowing a few electors to hold the balance of power in a close election, since some states might decide to appoint unpledged or expressly unbound electors. It would require the most tortured construction of the Constitution to give Congress the right to override the states that did this.

Sayre and Parris have another remedy for the faithless-elector problem, one that would place more responsibility on the political parties.

Voters in states where this happens are not always or even usually hapless victims. The election of maverick electors may be, at least in part, a fault of the system under which they were chosen by their party as members of a ticket—presumably without sufficient dissemination or understanding of their individual views. Any remedy would thus appear to be a logical and easily met responsibility of state and local party leaders.[44]

To some extent, then, Dr. Bailey's defection may have been the state's own fault. North Carolina had not exercised its right, under *Ray* v. *Blair*, to require political parties to pledge their nominees for the office of elector and to exclude those who refused to take such a pledge. Furthermore, Dr. Bailey's state political party did not carefully screen its nominees or discuss party loyalty and the nature

44. *Voting for President*, p. 137.

of their commitment with them. As Sayre and Parris recommend, the state party leaders themselves can minimize an already insignificant problem by carefully selecting nominees, requiring loyalty resolutions at party conventions, pledging each nominee, and using the sanctions of national patronage and campaign funds. Since "the failure to secure faithful electors has frequently been the result of insufficient attention on the part of national leaders,"[45] it would seem that these measures should be tried before the nation decides to take the route of a constitutional amendment.

A far more serious problem is illustrated by the case of Horace Greeley, the presidential candidate who died after the general election and before the meeting of the electoral college. Neither constitutional nor statutory law provides for the filling of vacancies that occur between party nomination and the day of the electoral-college vote. The Twenty-fifth Amendment deals with the President- and Vice-President-elect, who by definition are chosen by the electoral college, and not with the winner of the general election. The political parties have responded to the problem with resolutions passed by their national conventions empowering their national committees or a new convention to fill such a vacancy. The death or incapacity of a credible candidate poses a grave problem even prior to a general election, but it presents more serious difficulties after that election.

If a candidate who had won the general election died before the meeting of the electoral college, his party would

45. *Ibid.*, p. 149.

have to provide a new candidate for whom the winning electors could vote. In such a case the loyalty of the electors to their party would be of extreme importance. For this reason, if for no other, party officials should take every possible step to ensure the loyalty of their nominees for the office of elector. It may be argued that because of this potential problem a party should pick as its nominees ranking, active, national and state party leaders whose views and loyalty are known rather than unknown, inactive, low-ranking party members.

The benefits of securing faithful, responsible party leaders as electors might even extend to the present contingency-election procedure. It is an apparently inescapable fact that once the general election fails, some new effort to build a coalition must be undertaken. Coalition-making is in large part wheeling and dealing. Is there any reason to believe that deals are better if made in the House than if made by the candidates and their electors, especially if those electors are the very party leaders who would have had to choose a new candidate in the event of the original candidate's death? It is possible that electors who are state and national party leaders, party professionals, may be more representative of the presidential voting habits of the people than the House of Representatives. In the last six presidential elections the people have chosen a Republican President four times, but in only one of these elections did the congressmen they selected make up a Republican majority in the house. If the presidential candidates and their party-official electors could form a new coalition prior to the meeting of the electoral college, the members of the

House would be off the hook. The potential threat to the internal stability of the House itself would be eleminated, and the contest and the uncertainty would end quickly and decisively on the day the electoral college met. The President might be indebted to another candidate and his electors, but he would not be indebted to congressmen. As Zeidenstein points out, "This kind of indebtedness differs from that incurred with convention delegates or the electorate, in that the President's congressional creditors are (1) constantly on hand to demand payment by way of policy outcomes, and (2) are full-time political actors who interact with the President at the federal level."[46]

Perhaps the office of elector would have some utility if electors were national party professionals rather than nonentities. They might provide a means to avoid the problems of a House election. No contingency plan suggested to date is clearly satisfactory, and this proposal is no exception. But even if one believes that it is undesirable to continue the office of elector, the problem of faithless electors is miniscule, and the meager and technical benefits of eliminating the office do not justify the effort to pass a constitutional amendment.

46. Harvey Zeidenstein, *Direct Election of the President* (Lexington, Mass., 1973), p. 14.

6 Electoral Certainty

The premium for fraud is always great in close elections. In the 1960's the nation had two extremely close elections. In the 1960 race, charges and countercharges in several states marred the canvass and the count. The proponents of the direct-election plan believe that their reform would reduce the premium for fraud and chance created by the unit rule. In their view, the unit rule, which swings huge blocs of electoral votes from one candidate to another, increases the potential effects of fraud or of chance occurrences or even of simple errors in tabulation.

There is tremendous significance in a few popular votes in the large competitive states, and an entire election could hinge on a few popular votes in a few states. Advocates of direct election argue that because the potential effects are so great, the temptation to engage in fraud is intense. The argument is persuasive as far as it goes. But we must be careful to separate those defects which are intrinsic to the present system from those which are characteristic of any electoral system. In evaluating the potential for fraud in the present system, we must remember that close popular elections are converted by the unit rule itself into majorities in the electoral college. Close popular contests are not always close electoral contests. The electoral-vote percentages that the candidates obtain are never the same as their popular-vote percentages. This discrepancy ordinarily works to give the winner a higher electoral-vote percentage than his popular-vote percentage. In 1960, John Kennedy defeated Richard Nixon by a popular margin of 112,827 votes but with 56 percent of the electoral votes. It would have required a shift of votes in five diverse states to elect Nixon (Illinois, Missouri, New Mexico, Hawaii, and Nevada). Generally, the concerted action of several states is required to shift the victory in an election from one candidate to another. Under the electoral-count system each state is a separate unit, and any fraudulent activity, any election irregularity, affects only the votes of that particular state. For this reason Ernest Brown asserts that "the existing system isolates and insulates charges of voting irregularities."[1]

The losing candidate will not contest the election tallies in individual states unless it is possible to reverse the results in enough individual states to give him the election. In most cases, then, charges of irregularities have little significance for the candidates, since they will not affect the eventual result. In a few elections, however, a reversal of the results in a single state would have changed the outcome. In 1916, if Wilson had lost California, he would have lost the election. But in seven of the fifteen close elections between 1848 and 1968, a reversal in five to eight states would have been necessary to give the victory to the loser, and in

1. "Proposed Amendment a Power Vacuum for Political Blackmail," *Trial* 3 (June–July 1967), 15.

eleven of these close elections a reversal would have been necessary in at least three states.

The unit rule isolates and insulates charges of election irregularities, but it does not eliminate them. Such charges not only stain the legitimacy of the victor but also lead to recounts, litigation, and uncertainty. One objective of any electoral system is to create certainty, to reduce calls for recounts and for contests in the courts. There is a point, as L. Kinvin Wroth states, "where the interest in continuity in government must prevail even over the interest in an absolutely accurate result."[2] The question is whether the direct-election plan would reduce the premium for fraud and introduce a greater certainty into the electoral process. It might not. The potential for fraud arises when an election is very close. The unit rule distorts the election results to widen the margin of victory in the electoral count. Under the direct-election plan, the unit rule would be abolished; the number of actually close contests could be increased, and there would be greater incentive for the defeated candidate to demand a recount. Close elections breed contests. In the last one hundred years, the nation has had nine close popular races but only three close electoral races. In the closest popular contest in our history, in 1880, when Garfield defeated Hancock by 9,457 popular votes, or by 0.1 percent, Garfield won 57.9 percent of the electoral votes for a 15.8 percent electoral-vote margin over Hancock.

In 1968, there were approximately 167,000 voting pre-

2. "Election Contests and the Electoral Vote," *Dickinson Law Review* 65 (1961), 348.

cincts in the United States, 3,130 counties, fifty different sets of state electoral laws, and countless unwritten state practices. Direct election would expand the field for challenge. Instead of being confined to a few strategic states, the search for votes and for irregularities could be nationwide and could extend to every voting precinct. A margin of a few hundred thousand votes out of 70,000,000 might make the result less acceptable to the loser than a margin of 10 or 12 percent of the electoral votes. Instead of limiting contests to closely divided states, as the unit rule does, the direct-election plan opens the door to contests in any and every state. Twenty-five thousand fraudulent votes in Rhode Island or in Mississippi, which one candidate might have carried by a 60 or 70 percent margin, would be as significant as twenty-five thousand votes in closely divided California. And simple errors in tabulation, such as the transposition of figures in vote totals, can occur anywhere. If the defeated candidate called for recounts in isolated states where he had reason to believe irregularities worked to his detriment, the winning candidate would surely call for recounts in other states where he believed he could pick up some advantage.

The distortion created by the unit rule makes it more difficult for the loser to challenge the results in a close popular contest. The defeated candidate must pick up votes in particular states. It may well be more difficult to pick up five thousand to ten thousand votes in Missouri or Nevada than to pick up a hundred thousand votes in the country as a whole. The acceptability of the result to the defeated candidate is the key to election certainty. Once the loser has conceded, once he has accepted the results as definitive, the continuity of government is assured. But if he questions the results—if he fights on by means of recounts and litigation—doubts, delay, and even paralysis in government may follow.

It is not at all clear that recounts would be completed in the time interval between the November election and inauguration day, January 20. The swift resolution of contests depends on a number of factors, including individual state election-contest provisions, the perseverance of the contestant, and the delaying tactics adopted by his opponent. Senator Eagleton noted that in his state, Missouri, at least four weeks are required to verify and audit the election returns. Voting machines are used only in St. Louis and Kansas City; the rest of the state uses paper ballots.[3]

The 1960 contest in Hawaii demonstrates the problem of ensuring an accurate count and a swift recount. Two days after the election it appeared that Kennedy had won Hawaii by 102 votes. A later tabulation gave Hawaii to Nixon by 157 out of over 180,000 votes cast. Nixon's victory was then certified by the governer. However, Circuit Judge Jamieson ordered recounts, first in selected precincts, then in additional precincts, and finally in all precincts.[4] The recount was not completed until December 28, nine days after the electors had met. It gave the state to Ken-

3. *Congressional Quarterly* 28 (April 17, 1970), 1029.
4. U.S., Senate, Committee on the Judiciary, Subcommittee on Constitutional Amendments, *Hearings, Nomination and Election of President and Vice President and Qualifications for Voting,* 87th Cong., 1st sess., 1961, p. 413.

nedy by 115 votes out of more than 190,000. The governor then certified this result, and the Congress, proceeding in accordance with the Electoral Count Act of 1887, had to decide which of the two returns from Hawaii to count. Congress counted the votes of Hawaii's Democratic electors.

In 1960, Kennedy had won Illinois by about 9,000 votes out of 4,500,000. There were charges of vote fraud, particularly in Democratic Cook County. The Republican effort to uncover fraud in Illinois was dropped after it became apparent that an investigation could not be completed in time.[5] In a state the size of Illnois, it may be impossible to reach a final determination in the requisite time, and even if all contests could be resolved prior to the inauguration, having the presidential election suspended in limbo for a lengthy interval could create a serious crisis in the country, reduce the time available for an orderly transition of power, and result in a disputed presidential term. Once the public loses faith in the accuracy of the count, it may be difficult to restore public confidence.

In addition to calls for recounts and contests over the accuracy of the returns, the 40-percent rule of the direct-election plan might provoke recounts to determine whether any candidate had actually won 40 percent of the vote. In this type of contest, every vote, including those for minor candidates and write-in votes, would be significant, because each would be part of the total of which one candidate would have to win 40 percent. In this type of contest every ballot box and every voting machine would have to be ex-

5. Wroth, "Election Contests," p. 342.

amined. A direct election, then, might result in two contests: a contest to determine if anyone had won 40 percent of the vote and, if so, who; and, in the event that no one had, a contested runoff. Not only would the runner-up be likely to call for a recount to determine if, in fact, anyone had attained 40 percent, but minor candidates might well do so, because it is under a runoff that minor candidates have some leverage.

Delay and uncertainty add fuel to the fire of suspicion about the fairness of a count. Another factor which could fan the flame of suspicion under a direct-election plan is the potential diversity in requirements for registration and qualifications for voting. The joint resolution on direct election passed by the House gave the states the initiative in setting voter qualifications and gave Congress the reserve power to set uniform residence requirements for voting in presidential elections. The House bill also gave the states the initiative in prescribing the times, places, and manner of holding such elections and of determining entitlement to inclusion on the ballot, and again gave reserve power to Congress to make or alter such regulations.

But is reserve power enough? Logically, a direct popular vote requires uniform qualifications and regularity in counting practices. Although some of the proponents of the plan do not believe an amendment should order explicit national control over an election, many others are deeply troubled by the problem. Clarence Mitchell, speaking for the National Association for the Advancement of Colored People, stated that the plan would be acceptable to his organization *only* if there were "absolute and foolproof safe-

guards against discrimination in registering and in voting."[6]
A permanent, national voter-registration list and the national machinery to enforce it might serve; it has been suggested by several students of the electoral process, including Richard M. Scammon, who believes that "perhaps the
most important of all institutional barriers to voting are
our registration and residence requirements."[7] In a close
election the outcome could be affected by varied eligibility
requirements or by local vote-counting practices. While
Congress would have reserve power, we cannot predict
what circumstances would lead to its exercise, what degree
of diversity would cause Congress to act, or whether Congress would act swiftly once the necessity for action was
clear.

The problem is actually two-fold: one facet is uniform
voter qualifications which could be set by the Congress;
the other is federal administration of elections. Many congressmen are opposed to both, and the sponsors of the
amendment in both houses considered such proposals inexpedient. Senator Bayh voiced doubts that they could
ever persuade two-thirds of the Congress to agree to exclusive congressional control over voter qualifications, and
he believes that a national election-surveillance system

6. U.S., Senate, Committee on the Judiciary, Subcommittee on
Constitutional Amendments, *Hearings, Election of the President*,
89th Cong., 2d sess., and 90th Cong., 1st sess., 1968, p. 428 (cited
hereafter as 1968 Senate *Hearings*).

7. Richard M. Scammon, "The Electoral Process," *Law and
Contemporary Problems* 27 (1962), 299.

would be used as a whipping boy to defeat the entire measure.[8] Congressman Celler opposed two floor amendments designed to guarantee uniform national voting standards: "Since great powers are being taken away from the States, I think it would be suicidal—if I may use that term—to adopt either one of these amendments. By saying that, I do not express a view in disapproval of the theory. . . ."[9] The sponsors are probably correct, not only about the possibility of congressional approval, but also of state ratification.[10] Many state legislatures are jealous of their powers under the rising tide of nationalization. As Richard Claude has observed, "Nationalized politics rubs against the traditional legal grain because conducting elections and defining the scope of the franchise have generally been decentralized functions of state activity."[11]

Despite this tradition, the trend has been toward uniform standards, and Supreme Court decisions have added impetus to this process. In *South Carolina* v. *Katzenbach,* the Court upheld sections of the Voting Rights Act of 1965, finding that Congress had the power to abolish voting tests in areas where an unacceptable percentage of residents of voting age have registered or voted in a presidential election, in order to effectuate the prohibition against racial

8. 1968 Senate *Hearings,* pp. 379, 511.

9. *Congressional Record,* Vol. 115, Pt. 19, 91st Cong., 1st sess. (1969), p. 25980.

10. Edwin Eshleman and Robert S. Walker, "Congress and Electoral Reform," *Christian Century* 86 (Feb. 5, 1969), 180.

11. "Nationalization of the Electoral Process," *Harvard Journal on Legislation* 6 (Jan. 1969), 140.

discrimination in voting in the Fifteenth Amendment.[12] In *Katzenbach* v. *Morgan*, the Court ruled that Section 4 (e) of the same act was constitutional; Justice William Brennan, writing for the majority, agreed that Congress had the power to override a state literacy requirement pursuant to enforcing the equal-protection clause of the Fourteenth Amendment.[13] In *Williams* v. *Rhodes*, the Court for the first time ruled that the state power, under Article II, Section 1, to select presidential electors is limited by the Fourteenth Amendment. Justice Hugo Black, for the majority, rejected the argument that Ohio had a compelling interest in the promotion of a two-party system and in the prevention of plurality victories which justified the burdens it placed on third parties desiring a place on the ballot.[14]

The process of setting standards through the courts is often slower than through the Congress and is accomplished on a case-by-case basis. *Williams*, for example, was not strong on guidelines for the states. As Chief Justice Warren pointed out in his dissent, "The opinion of this Court . . . leaves unresolved what restrictions, if any, a state can impose."[15] In fact, *Williams* may have raised more questions than it answered. John H. Barton notes that it is not yet clear whether it will be applied only to third parties or also to factional candidates who splinter the major parties.

Under any doctrine, the Court will have to inquire whether

12. 383 U.S. 301 (1965).
13. 384 U.S. 641 (1966).
14. 393 U.S. 23 (1968).
15. 393 U.S. 69 (1968).

particular groups deserve independent ballot representation. The case of the American Independent Party is clear enough, but what about a dissident major-party faction that does not like its party's nominees or a black-power party with racially restricted membership?[16]

In order to avoid a crisis, it appears essential that uniform provisions for voter qualification and registration, for access to the ballot, and for the counting procedure be established and be in effect prior to a direct popular election. The necessity for instituting provisions prior to the election is one lesson that should have been learned from the turmoil of 1876.

Federal guidelines are one thing; federal surveillance is another. Under *McPherson* v. *Blacker*, the state legislatures do not have to institute a popular election.[17] They may appoint the electors themselves. The choice of method is theirs. But if they choose election by the people, the body of case law suggests that the First, Fourteenth, Fifteenth, Nineteenth, and Twenty-sixth Amendments place limitations on the states.[18] "Short of compromising judicially defined First Amendment rights and constitutional voting rights where race and fair representation are concerned,"

16. John H. Barton, "The General Election Ballot: More Nominees or More Representative Nominees?" *Stanford Law Review* 22 (Jan. 1970), 167.

17. 146 U.S. 1 (1892).

18. Donald M. Wilkinson, Jr., "The Electoral Process and the Power of the States," *American Bar Association Journal* 47 (1961), 251; James C. Kirby, Jr., "Limitations on the Power of State Legislatures over Presidential Elections," *Law and Contemporary Problems* 27 (1962), 495–509; Claude, "Nationalization of the Electoral Process," p. 139.

Richard Claude concludes, "there appear few barriers left standing to impede Congress from doing what it thinks appropriate to enforce equal protection guarantees applicable to the conduct of any election."[19] Thus Congress already has vast potential authority over the presidential-election process. The reserve power granted to the Congress under the proposed amendment does not so much extend this power as reaffirm it.

Although the trend may be toward nationalization of the electoral process, through Supreme Court rulings and congressional guidelines, the tradition of decentralized administration of elections remains strong. Despite this tradition, many believe that federal administration of presidential elections would be either inevitable or absolutely necessary under the direct-election plan. Robert Dixon, for example, observes that local corruption in vote-counting stands in the way of a happy conversion to a direct, all-national election. Local corruption has some effects on the present system but, as Dixon has argued, "under direct popular voting the impact would be immediate, direct and national."[20] Therefore federal administration of elections would be necessary to guarantee open, honest unintimidated balloting and an accurate count. William T. Gossett, of the American Bar Association, agreed that nationally supervised elections might become necessary.[21]

19. Claude, "Nationalization of the Electoral Process," p. 160.

20. Robert G. Dixon, Jr., *Democratic Representation* (New York, 1968), p. 571.

21. U.S., House of Representatives, Committee on the Judiciary, *Hearings, Electoral College Reform*, 91st Cong., 1st sess., 1969, p. 197.

Aside from pre-emption of the state power to conduct elections, there are other problems with federal administration that produce grave misgivings. Opponents cite the possibility of manipulation and the opportunity for abuse inherent in a centralized administration. Yet, the problem of local corruption in the count is not insignificant, as Theodore H. White reports:

Those who report elections know, alas, that the mores and morality of vote-counting vary from state to state. The votes of Minnesota, California, Wisconsin and half a dozen other states are as honorably collected and counted as votes anywhere in the world. There are other states in the Union where votes are bought, paid for and, in all too many cases, counted, manipulated and miscounted by thieves. The voting results of the valley counties of Texas are a scandal; so, too, are the voting results in scores of precincts of Illinois' Cook County; so too, in ward after ward of West Virginia, in the hills of Tennessee and Kentucky, and in dozens of other pockets of rural or urban machine-controlled slums.[22]

L. Kinvin Wroth contends that the problems of greatest importance are not those relating to voter qualifications but rather "those concerning the manner in which the popular vote is given, counted, canvassed and communicated to the Congress."[23]

If national surveillance of the electoral process is unsatisfactory because centralized administration increases the potential for manipulation, and if under a direct election where all the votes are pooled, close elections might lead

22. *The Making of the President, 1968* (New York, 1969), p. 407.
23. Wroth, "Election Contests," p. 323.

to contests and recounts—perhaps even to competition in corruption, with vote stealers matching their skills, as they did in the election of 1876—then there is something to be said for the present federal system. There is something to be said for a system that magnifies the margin of victory, thus making the decision clearer, more difficult to challenge, and therefore more acceptable to the losing candidate. There is something to be said for a system that sharply limits the number of votes likely to be contested, that compartmentalizes and separates the votes of honest and dishonest states.

The American presidential-election system has a legitimizing function. The election is the nation's method for determining who its rightful leaders will be. But uncertainty undercuts legitimacy, and there is no reason to believe the direct-election plan would increase the certainty in any close election.

7 A Federal System or an Assembly of the Whole?

> Transfer of power is best coped with by means the re-
> gime has incorporated through time and proven in prac-
> tice.
>
> Myron Rush

This analysis and evaluation of the current attempts to reform the presidential election process by instituting a direct popular election indicates that the reform is not merely "a housekeeping item"[1] on the agenda of the American people but would be a fundamental change in our governmental system. The reformers are correct in concluding that the present method has defects. Despite the proponents' claims, the direct-election plan is not a panacea. There are serious contraindications which should give us pause, for the remedy may be worse than the disease.

Although the proponents of the direct-election plan appear to have a strong case against the existing system, the appearance is not the reality. Their case abstracts from political practice and is at once too mechanical and mathe-

1. Neal Peirce, *The People's President: The Electoral College in American History and the Direct Vote Alternative* (New York, 1968), p. 296.

matical. The nation may be better advised to follow the advice of its first president: "Experience is the surest standard by which to test the real tendency of [a] constitution." In their indictment, the critics charge that the existing system does not guarantee victory to the plurality winner, because the runner-up may be elected either in the electoral college or in a House contingency election. Their case against the existing contingency procedure is almost wholly refuted by the fact that the country has never had nor is likely to have one under the unit rule, as experience with close elections and third-party candidates makes evident. The electoral-count system magnifies the plurality winner's margin of victory unless his appeal is sectionally concentrated and thus insures the victory of the candidate with broad appeal.

Despite this evidence, many critics look for trouble and rely on the shift-in-votes argument to support their contention that the existing system could frequently produce a runner-up President. The shift-in-votes-argument fails because it rests on the manipulation of numbers rather than of voters. It is simple to move an exact and limited number of votes from one paper column to another in a political vacuum; it is more difficult to move an exact *and limited* number of voters from one candidate to another in the political world. In many instances the shift-in-votes argument ignores the election laws and therefore cannot be considered a critique of the present system but of an imaginary system designed to fit the predictions of the critics.

Not only do the critics ignore the election laws, but they also disregard the role of the political parties, which, because of their power preoccupation, have adapted themselves to the system and have, in the main, reinforced it by seeking broad cross-sectional rather than sectional bases of support. Unless we abstract from the "historic achievement" of the political parties, a runner-up President is not likely. The possibility of a runner-up Presidency or of a contingency election looms larger in theory than in practice. The existing system has persistently and consistently reinforced the results of the popular election, and it has attached a federal-geographic rider to the rule of the simple arithmetical majority, a rider which attempts to secure a President who represents the nation in its diversity.

The electoral-count system is not neutral; it has a built-in bias in favor of the two-party system, since it discriminates against both sectional and national third parties. The built-in necessity to win broad, cross-national support may have a tempering effect on the character of the two major parties. It is generally believed that the major parties are moderate and nonideological. Whether the electoral system is the "cause" of this phenomenon is debatable, but it clearly supports moderation by giving the parties the incentive to create broad, cross-national coalitions.

The second major charge in the critics' indictment is that the present system produces severe inequalities in individual voting power. They point to the distortions in voting power that arise because electoral votes are distributed among the states according to the decennial census and because voter turnout may vary from state to state. A direct election would eliminate these factors, but it would also break the links between the congressional and the presidential constituencies. The "lost-vote" argument—that votes for the intrastate losing candidate are misappropriated, given to the candidate intrastate minority voters oppose—actually begs the question. It amounts to little more than the statement that the President is not currently elected by a direct vote of the people but, rather, by a federally aggregated majority or plurality of the people. The question is not whether the federal principle is used as a jurisdictional basis for presidential elections, but whether it should be. But the case against federalism has not been made. If and when it is, we should consider abandoning it for the national legislature as well as the executive. Until then, there is reason to conclude that federalism may be appropriate for a continental, heterogeneous nation.

The existing system creates certain advantages for particular groups of voters, which have a bearing on public policy and its formation. Under this system large competitive states have an advantage. It may be argued that they should be the primary battlegrounds for the Presidency, since they may best represent the nation in its diversity. The system also creates advantages for urban-suburban voters and well-organized urban minorities. The Presidency has been sensitive to urban and minority interests—according to some political analysts, because the parties have perceived the urban-ethnic advantage and taken it into consideration in selecting candidates and issues. To the extent that Congress has a rural–small-town bias, this Presidential sensitivity to urban-ethnic problems provides a desirable balance.

In the final analysis the voter-inequality argument fails

because its perspective on equality is too narrow and apolitical. Even giving each voter an absolutely equally weighted vote for the President would not ensure absolute voter equality, for the Presidency is but one of the power centers in the nation. Nor can absolute individual voter equality be equated with political equality, because such an equation disregards the intensity of preferences, the effects of noncompulsory voting, the fact of group organization, and the necessity to build coalitions in a pluralistic nation.

The remaining charges in the indictment are either insignificant or not exclusive to the existing system. The faithless-elector problem is not only miniscule, but it might be mitigated if the political parties exercised greater care and responsibility in selecting their nominees for the office of elector. Fraud is a problem for all electoral systems and is particularly threatening in a close election. There is reason to believe that the direct-election method would increase rather than reduce the dangers of fraud, because it would increase the number of actually close elections. Under the direct-election contingency provisions, fraud might occur in two elections, the general election and the runoff.

The consequences of the existing system are known and reassuring; the consequences of the direct-election plan are not known and must be merely the objects of speculation. There are general standards for judging the health of any electoral plan; the known consequences of the existing system may be compared to the best assessment of the probable consequences of the proposed plan in the light of those standards.

First, an electoral system should produce a definite, accepted winner and avoid prolonged contests and disputes that create uncertainty and public turmoil. Our present electoral system passes this test, partly because of the electoral rules and partly because of customs. It has proven itself in time and practice. There have been no contingency elections since the adoption of the unit rule. Only one election has been seriously disputed because of fraud. On the other hand the direct election could provoke contests and disputes, and it would necessitate national voter lists and federal administration of elections. Contrary to the proponents' suggestion, the 40-percent runoff rule could make frequent resort to a contingency election necessary. Once the unit rule, with its bias in favor of the two major-party candidates, is abolished, the 40-percent runoff rule could serve as an open invitation to multiple candidacies and thereby facilitate a contingency-election strategy. If the unit rule were abandoned, concern about fraud would not be limited to key states but, rather, could extend to the whole nation, compounding delay and uncertainty.

Second, an electoral system should preserve the prestige, power, and potential for leadership of the office of the President. The present system is unquestionably healthy on this score. Under its rules, the Presidency has become the focal point of the government. It has grown and developed to a degree that would have astounded the Founders. But there is reason to doubt that the power of the Presidency ought to be enhanced, particularly in the current political climate, in which voices are being raised against "the imperial Presidency." Yet, if disputes and contests could be contained, the direct-election plan would extend and increase the Presidency's power and potential for leadership. A plebiscitary Presidency as a symbol of the general will would strengthen the position of the President in relation to Congress, which cannot claim to speak clearly for the general will but only for concurrent majorities or pluralities. The direct-election plan is part of a trend toward centralization—a trend, James Burnham contends, whose "end is Caesar."[2] This trend may result in the weakening of the intermediary institutions that have served the republic well.

The intermediary institutions always appear to be incomplete, distorted and obstructive expressions of the general will. Through them are expressed the interests of classes, local regions, industries, churches, races, or other sub-sections of the people as a whole. Not only do the intermediary institutions appear in this way partial. The appearance is not deceptive: it is a fact that they are expressions of only parts or elements of the general will and interest. It is precisely through these intermediary institutions that the otherwise formless, politically meaningless, abstract entity, "the people," is given structure, and becomes articulate, organized, and operationally significant.[3]

This pluralistic nation may be better served by its system of concurrent majorities than by a system that would make the President the embodiment of the general will, the plebiscitary leader who speaks for no special interest.

Furthermore, direct election would have a profound effect on the kinds of men who would become President. If,

2. *Congress and the American Tradition* (Chicago, 1959), p. 296.
3. *Ibid.*, p. 297.

as this analysis has suggested, the direct-election plan would change or even destroy the national party-convention system, professional party leaders could lose control over the nomination process. Their loss of control might result in a new breed of candidates, candidates who under the present system would not be politically eligible. Demagogues, self-nominated, individualistic leaders of impermanent factions, charismatic leaders riding a single issue might replace the candidates presently recruited because of their moderation, experience, records of electoral success, and service to permanent party organizations.

Third, an electoral system should support our nonideological two-party system. The present electoral-count procedure has nurtured and protected that two-party system. Direct election would alter or erode this system, which "more than any other American Institution, consciously, actively and directly nurtures consensus."[4] Once the unit rule, which discriminates against third and fourth candidacies, is abolished, party convention control over nominations would break down, since candidates would not have to win statewide pluralities. Multiple candidacies might be common, since each new candidacy in itself would be an incentive for the entry of another. The more candidates, the more likely a runoff. The second chance that a runoff provides is tempting, not only because of its effect on candidates' perceptions of their prospects, but also because of its effect on voter psychology. If nominating the President is the key function of the national parties and perhaps even

4. Austin Ranney and Willmore Kendall, *Democracy and the American Party System* (New York, 1956), p. 508.

their reason for being, as many political analysts have suggested, direct election would emasculate, if not destroy, the two-party system by breaking down party control over nominations. By abandoning the unit rule, which has acted as a goad, prodding the parties to broaden their appeal and widen their bases of support, the direct-election system would release latent tendencies toward ideological politics. The prospects are that the direct-election plan would increase the incidence of party splits, encourage the development of minor parties, undermine party control over the crucial task of nomination, postpone compromise, simplify and dramatize issues, increase the importance of homogeneous regions and one-party states, disturb the geographic distribution of party support, reduce the influence of state party leaders, and encourage the formation of doctrinaire and single-issue parties. Even if the unit rule is not a major pillar of the presidential two-party system, even if, instead, the two-party system is mainly supported by noninstitutional factors, by "a happy balance struck between consensus and conflict,"[5] the present turmoil in the nation, the present degree of conflict, indicates this is no time to kick away the institutional props, for, as Allan Sindler concludes, two-partyism is still a mystery, and "institutional arrangements, even if secondary, also shape the party system; and both categories complement rather than compete in their effects."[6]

Fourth, an electoral system should preserve federalism.

5. Allan Sindler, *Political Parties in the United States* (New York, 1966), p. 58.
6. *Ibid.*, p. 59.

The present system fortifies federalism by making the states the crucial political units in the selection of the President, both by giving coalitions of state and local party leaders great influence in the nomination process and by requiring statewide victories in the election itself. The direct-election plan would change this by scuttling the nominating conventions and by making state lines irrelevant in the general-election contest. Candidates would be liberated from their bonds of dependence on state and local party organizations, since they could be self-nominated factional leaders or proposed by transient quasi-political groups. They would be able to select their own constituencies with greater freedom, carving them out of the states, replacing geographic with issue-oriented constituencies. Paul Freund, a supporter of the direct-election plan, admits that if the "reform is adopted, the federal character of presidential elections will be significantly affected; the countervailing distortions in the present procedure will be removed and the value inhering in the federal nature of the parties themselves must be supported by other means."[7]

Finally, an electoral system should provide effective representation and political equality. The present system does not provide arithmetical equality; it does not provide each voter with an equally weighted vote. Political equality, however, involves much more than the strictly logical application of an oversimplified principle. Political equality and effective representation can mean each member has an

7. Paul Freund, "The Supreme Court and the Future of Federalism," in *The Future of Federalism*, ed. Samuel Shuman (Detroit, 1968), p. 47.

opportunity to participate in the total decision-making process.[8] More is involved than "the self-centered constitutional right of a voter to cast a vote which, at least in mathematical, non-functional terms, is weighted equally with the votes of others."[9]

Under the existing presidential election system, the Presidency has become increasingly sensitive to urban minority interests, interests which have been neglected elsewhere. The political system, considered as a whole, is one which reflects the views and interests of broad cross sections of the country. It is a system of concurrent majorities in which each major interest has some access to the centers of power. The direct-election plan would change the balance in the present power system. It would change the balance against those very interests which have the greatest need for access to the power structure. The price we must pay to purify our system to make it more logically consistent with the principle of majoritarian democracy may be too high. What we gain may not be worth the cost. Moreover, it is questionable whether direct election would necessarily fulfill the requirements of majoritarian democracy. The direct-election plan would not even meet its own standards of popular sovereignty and majority rule unless there were but two alternative candidates from whom to choose. Unless the two-party system is an independent variable, unaffected by institutional forms, we cannot assume its continued survival and vigor under direct election. As Sayre

8. Ranney, *Democracy*, p. 28.
9. Robert G. Dixon, Jr., *Democratic Representation* (New York, 1968), p. 19.

and Parris point out, "The burden of proof lies heavily upon those who would eliminate known defects of the electoral college system but risk the hazards of untested alternatives."[10] Because the proponents of direct election assume two-party competition, they clearly have not borne the burden of proof.

The argument for the retention of the electoral-college system rests on existing knowledge about our political order as a whole and about the kinds of problems that political order has attempted to resolve. It rests on the judgment that ours is a Madisonian system of concurrent majorities designed to check majority factions that lead to majority tyranny. It rests on the judgment that political institutions are intimately related to the environment that nourishes them, and on the Aristotelian principle that viable regimes are not created in the abstract or established by fiat but, rather, are organisms that grow out of the environment in which they are rooted. Finally, it rests on the judgment that the best way to assess an institution (like the best way to judge a man) is to determine what it does—its practical effects.

The present electoral system is not perfect. To cure all its defects may be beyond present skill. The possibility of a runner-up Presidency continues to plague us. Its incidence, however, has been very infrequent, and since it is directly related to an improper vote-distribution pattern, it may not be foolhardy to rely on our power-oriented major

10. Wallace S. Sayre and Judith H. Parris, *Voting for President: The Electoral College and the American Political System* (Washington, 1972), p. 2.

parties to prevent and limit a recurrence. Indeed, the prospect of a runner-up Presidency, the prospect of winning the popular but not the electoral vote, spurs those parties to seek the support of broad cross sections of the nation. The risk of a runner-up Presidency may not be too great a price to pay for a system which minimizes conflicts, promises stability, suppresses factions, promotes moderation, and requires a broad base of support.

Our governmental system was instituted and has evolved to maintain the uneasy tension between majority rule and political liberty. Thus our system is not logically pure and consistent; it is devoted to two often contradictory principles. We have found it in our interest to maintain this tension, because "counting heads expresses the will of the people well enough only so long as the heads are all much alike, only so long as the minority is willing to accept the decision of the majority and let it go at that."[11] In this large and diverse nation the heads are not all much alike, and some minorities are not willing to accept the decision of the majority when their fundamental interests are affected. Our solution to the problem of conflicting goals has been a system of concurrent majorities, a system which attempts to give every major interest some voice in the policy decisions with which it is most directly concerned. Our Madisonian system has been viable because it attempts to reflect the views and interests of broad cross sections of the polity. Those who support this Madisonian system recognize, as some of the supporters of the direct-election

11. Carl Becker, "The Will of the People," *Yale Review* 34 (March 1945), 391.

218 The Case Against Direct Election

plan do not, that politics is not an exact science, that "man is a political animal, as well as a census statistic."[12]

The electoral-count system has been, on the whole, a success. It has never failed to fill the office of President. In every election since the universal adoption of the unit rule, it has given us a single election. It has provided a constitutionally elected and constitutionally recognized President, even on the verge of civil war. It has given the victory to the winner of the popular plurality in every case but one, despite a series of strong third-party threats, particularly in this century. It has nurtured a moderate two-party system. Under its rules, the Presidency has grown in both power and prestige.

Judged in terms of its practical effects, our electoral system has a sound heart. Like all living things, it has imperfections and defects, but it functions; indeed, it thrives. Those who focus on its blemishes, real or imagined, advocate major surgery in the pursuit of abstract perfection, preferring logical consistency to viability. Major surgery is not indicated if we prefer life to logic.

12. Dixon, *Democratic Representation*, p. 22.

Bibliography

Congressional Documents

Senate, Committee on the Judiciary, Subcommittee on Constitutional Amendments, *Hearings, Nomination and Election of President and Vice President and Qualifications for Voting*, 87th Congress, 1st session, 1961.

Senate, Committee on the Judiciary, Subcommittee on Constitutional Amendments, *Hearings, Nomination and Election of President and Vice President*, 88th Congress, 1st session, 1963.

Senate, Committee on the Judiciary, Subcommittee on Constitutional Amendments, *Hearings, Election of the President*, 89th Congress, 2d session, and 90th Congress, 1st session, 1968.

House of Representatives, Committee on the Judiciary, *Hearings, Electoral College Reform*, 91st Congress, 1st session, 1969.

Senate, Committee on the Judiciary, Subcommittee on Constitutional Amendments, *Hearings, Electing the President*, 91st Congress, 1st session, 1969.

Senate, Committee on the Judiciary, *Hearings, Electoral College Reform*, 91st Congress, 2d session, 1970.

Books

American Bar Association, *Electing the President: A Report of the Commission on Electoral College Reform*. Chicago: 1967.

Bickel, Alexander. *The New Age of Political Reform.* New York: Harper and Row, 1968.

Book of States. Chicago: Council of State Governments, 1968.

Burnham, James. *Congress and the American Tradition.* Chicago: Regnery, 1959.

Burns, James MacGregor. *The Deadlock of Democracy.* Englewood Cliffs, N.J.: Prentice-Hall, 1965.

Campbell, Angus, *et al. The American Voter.* New York: Wiley, 1964.

Corwin, Edward. *The President, Office and Powers.* New York: New York University Press, 1957.

Counting Electoral Votes: Proceedings and Debates of Congress Relating to Counting the Electoral Votes for President and Vice President of the United States. Washington: Government Printing Office, 1877.

Dahl, Robert A. *A Preface to Democratic Theory.* Chicago: University of Chicago Press, 1956.

David, Paul T. *The Politics of National Party Conventions.* New York: Random House, 1964.

Dixon, Robert G., Jr. *Democratic Representation.* New York: Oxford University Press, 1968.

Dougherty, J. Hampden. *The Electoral System of the United States.* New York: Putnam's, 1906.

Eidelberg, Paul. *The Philosophy of the American Constitution.* New York: Free Press, 1968.

Ewing, Cortez. *Presidential Elections.* Norman: University of Oklahoma Press, 1940.

Goldwin, Robert A., ed. *Representation and Misrepresentation.* Chicago: Rand McNally, 1968.

Hamilton, Alexander, John Jay, and James Madison. *The Federalist Papers.* Ed. Clinton Rossiter. New York: New American Library, 1961.

Haworth, Paul L. *The Hayes-Tilden Disputed Presidential Election of 1876.* Cleveland: Burrows, 1906.

Hesseltine, William B. *Third Party Movements in the United States.* New York: Van Nostrand, 1962.

James, Judson. *American Political Parties: Potential and Performance.* New York: Western, 1969.

Key, V. O. *Southern Politics.* New York: Random House, 1949.

MacBride, Roger Lea. *The American Electoral College.* Caldwell, Idaho: Caxton Printers, 1953.

MacMahon, Arthur W., ed. *Federalism Mature and Emergent.* New York: Doubleday, 1955.

Matthews, Donald R., ed. *Perspectives on Presidential Selection.* Washington: Brookings Institution, 1973.

McKnight, David A. *The Electoral System of the United States.* Philadelphia: Lippincott, 1878.

Neustadt, Richard E. *Presidential Power.* New York: New American Library, 1964.

O'Neill, Charles A. *The American Electoral System.* New York: Putnam's, 1887.

Peirce, Neal R. *The People's President: The Electoral College in American History and the Direct Vote Alternative.* New York: Simon and Schuster, 1968.

Petersen, Svend. *A Statistical History of the American Presidential Elections.* New York: Ungar, 1968.

Phillips, Kevin P. *The Emerging Republican Majority.* New Rochelle, N.Y.: Arlington House, 1969.

Polsby, Nelson, and Aaron B. Wildavsky. *Presidential Elections: Strategies of American Electoral Politics.* New York: Scribner's, 1964.

Pomper, Gerald. *Nominating the President: The Politics of Convention Choice.* New York: Norton, 1966.

Ranney, Austin, and Willmore Kendall. *Democracy and the American Party System.* New York: Harcourt, Brace, 1956.

Ripon Society. *The Lessons of Victory*. New York: Dial Press, 1969.

Roseboom, Eugene. *A Short History of Presidential Elections*. New York: Macmillan, 1967.

Rossiter, Clinton. *The American Presidency*. New York: New American Library, 1964.

——. *Parties and Politics in America*. Ithaca: Cornell University Press, 1967.

Sayre, Wallace S., and Judith H. Parris. *Voting for President: The Electoral College and the American Political System*. Washington: Brookings Institution, 1972.

Schattschneider, E. E. *Party Government*. New York: Holt, Rinehart and Winston, 1967.

——. *The Semi-Sovereign People*. New York: Holt, Rinehart and Winston, 1960.

Schwartz, Bernard. *A Commentary on the Constitution of the United States: Powers of the President*. New York: Macmillan, 1963.

Shuman, Samuel, ed. *The Future of Federalism*. Detroit: Wayne State University Press, 1968.

Sindler, Allan P. *Political Parties in the United States*. New York: Saint Martin's Press, 1966.

Stanwood, Edward. *A History of Presidential Elections*. Boston: Osgood, 1884.

——. *A History of the Presidency*. Boston: Houghton Mifflin, 1898.

Tocqueville, Alexis de. *Democracy in America*. Ed. Richard D. Heffner. New York: New American Library, 1956.

Tugwell, Rexford. *How They Became President*. New York: Simon and Schuster, 1968.

Valeo, Francis, Richard C. Hupman, and Robert Tienken. *Nomination and Election of the President and Vice President of the United States: Including the Manner of Selecting Delegates to National Political Conventions*. Washington: Government Printing Office, 1968.

Venetoulis, Theodore G. *The House Shall Choose.* Margate, N.J.: Elias Press, 1968.

Wechsler, Herbert. *Principles, Politics and Fundamental Law.* Cambridge, Mass.: Harvard University Press, 1961.

White, Theodore H. *The Making of the President, 1960.* New York: New American Library, 1967.

———. *The Making of the President, 1964.* New York: New American Library, 1966.

———. *The Making of the President, 1968.* New York: Atheneum, 1969.

Wilmerding, Lucius. *The Electoral College.* New Brunswick, N.J.: Rutgers University Press, 1958.

The World Almanac, 1970. New York: Newspaper Enterprise Association, 1970.

Zeidenstein, Harvey. *Direct Election of the President.* Lexington, Mass.: Heath, 1973.

Articles

Andrews, William G. "American Voting Participation." *Western Political Quarterly* 19 (1966), 639.

———. "Three Electoral Colleges." *Parliamentary Affairs* 14 (1960–1961), 178.

Auerbach, Carl A. "The Reapportionment Cases: One Person, One Vote—One Vote, One Value." *Supreme Court Review,* 1964, p. 1.

Banzhaf, John F., III. "One Man, 3.312 Votes: A Mathematical Analysis of the Electoral College." *Villanova Law Review* 13 (Winter 1968), 303.

Barton, John H. "The General Election Ballot: More Nominees or More Representative Nominees?" *Stanford Law Review* 22 (Jan. 1970), 165.

Bayh, Birch. "Comment." *Villanova Law Review* 13 (Winter 1968), 331.

———. "Electing a President: The Case for Direct Popular Election." *Harvard Journal on Legislation* 6 (Jan. 1969), 127.

Becker, Carl. "The Will of the People." *Yale Review* 34 (March 1945), 385.

Bickel, Alexander. "The Case for the Electoral College." *New Republic* 156 (Jan. 28, 1967), 15.

———. "Is Electoral Reform the Answer?" *Commentary* 46 (July–Dec. 1968), 41.

———. "The Popular Election of Future Presidents: Wait A Minute!" *New Republic* 160 (May 10, 1969), 11.

Bogardus, Emory S. "The Electoral College as a Sociopolitical Institution." *Sociology and Social Research* 45 (April 1961), 332.

Boyd, William J. D. "Suburbia Takes Over." *National Civic Review* 54 (1965), 294.

Brown, Ernest. "Proposed Amendment a Power Vacuum for Political Blackmail." *Trial* 3 (June–July 1967), 15.

Buckles, Frederick. "Electoral College Reform: The Proposals and Prospects." *St. Louis University Law Journal* 14 (Fall 1969), 121.

Burns, James MacGregor. "A New Course for the Electoral College." *New York Times Magazine*, Dec. 18, 1960, p. 10.

Carlisle, J. G. "Dangerous Defects in Our Electoral System." *The Forum* 24 (Nov. 1897), 257.

Claude, Richard. "Nationalization of the Electoral Process." *Harvard Journal on Legislation* 6 (Jan. 1969), 139.

De Grazia, Alfred. "General Theory of Apportionment." *Law and Contemporary Problems* 17 (1952), 256.

Dixon, Robert G., Jr. "Electoral College Procedure." *Western Political Quarterly* 3 (1950), 214.

Dolan, Joseph F. "How We Elect Our President: An Electoral College Education in One Lesson." *American Bar Association Journal* 42 (1956), 1037.

Drucker, Peter F. "A Key to Calhoun's Pluralism." *Review of Politics* 10 (1948), 412.

Dye, Thomas R. "Malapportionment and Public Policy in the States." *Journal of Politics* 27 (1965), 587.

Eagan, Emmett E., Jr. "Constitutional Law, Elections, Equal Protection." *Case Western Reserve Law Review* 20 (1969), 892.

"Electing Presidents." *New Republic* 160 (Feb. 22, 1969), 9.

"Electoral Reform." *New Republic* 160 (March 15, 1969), 10.

Eshleman, Edwin, and Robert S. Walker. "Congress and Electoral Reform." *Christian Century* 86 (Feb. 5, 1969), 178.

Farrelly, David G., and Ivan Hinderaker. "Congressional Reapportionment and National Political Power." *Law and Contemporary Problems* 17 (1952), 339.

Ford, Gerald A. "A Ballot for Electoral College Reform." *Trial* 5 (Dec.–Jan. 1968–1969), 49.

Goldman, Ralph. "Hubert Humphrey's, S.J. 152: A New Proposal for Electoral College Reform." *Midwest Journal of Political Science* 2 (1958), 89.

Hamilton, John A. "The Ox-Cart Way We Pick a Space-Age President." *New York Times Magazine*, Oct. 20, 1968, p. 36.

Heinlein, J. C. "Presidential Election Procedure." *University of Cincinnati Law Review* 35 (Winter 1966), 1.

Hill, A. Spenser. "The Reapportionment Decisions: A Return to Dogma." *Journal of Politics* 31 (1969), 186.

Hofferbert, Richard I. "The Relation between Public Policy and Some Structural and Environmental Variables in the American States." *American Political Science Review* 60 (1966), 73.

"How Not to Elect a President." *Time* 95 (May 4, 1970), 26.

Johnson, Gerald W. "Leave the College Alone." *New Republic* 144 (Jan. 9, 1961), 22.

Joyner, Conrad, and Ronald Pedderson. "The Electoral College Revisited." *Southwestern Social Science Quarterly* 45 (June 1964), 26.

Kallenbach, Joseph. "Our Electoral College Gerrymander." *Midwest Journal of Political Science* 4 (1960), 162.

Kateb, George. "The Majority Principle: Calhoun and His Antecedents." *Political Science Quarterly* 84 (1969), 583.

Kefauver, Estes. "The Electoral College: Old Reforms Take on a New Look." *Law and Contemporary Problems* 27 (1962), 188.

Kelly, Stanley, Jr., Richard E. Ayres, and William Bowen. "Registration and Voting: Putting First Things First." *American Political Science Review* 61 (1967), 359.

Keogh, Eugene J. "Shall We Abolish the Electoral College?" *Brooklyn Bar* 4 (April 1953), 173.

Kirby, James C., Jr. "Limitations on the Power of State Legislatures over Presidential Elections." *Law and Contemporary Problems* 27 (1962), 495.

——. "Turmoil on the Electoral College Campus." *The Progressive* 32 (Oct. 1968), 13.

Kozusko, Donald, and Paul J. Lambert. "The Uncertain Impact of *Williams* v. *Rhodes* on Qualifying Minority Parties for the Ballot." *Harvard Journal on Legislation* 6 (Jan. 1969), 236.

Krastin, Karl. "The Implementation of Representative Government in a Democracy." *Iowa Law Review* 48 (1963), 549.

Krislov, Samuel. "The Electoral College." *Parliamentary Affairs* 11 (1957–1958), 466.

Kristol, Irving, and Paul Weaver. "A Bad Idea Whose Time Has Come." *New York Times Magazine*, Nov. 23, 1969, p. 43.

Le Maistre, George A. "May Presidential Electors Be Bound?" *Journal of Public Law* 1 (Fall 1952), 348.

Lewis, Anthony. "An Amendment to Catch up with History." *New York Times*, Sept. 21, 1969, p. 14.

Lewis, Walker. "The Hayes-Tilden Election Contest." *American Bar Association Journal* 47 (1961), 36.

Lugg, Harry H. "State Legislatures' Authority over the Selection of Presidential Electors." *Connecticut Bar Journal* 37 (1963), 7.

Patterson, Kirby W. "A Responsible Presidency: Suggestion for a New Method of Selection." *American Bar Association Journal* 38 (1952), 551.

Peirce, Neal. "The Case against the Electoral College." *New Republic* 156 (Feb. 11, 1967), 12.

——. "The Electoral College Goes to Court." *The Reporter* 35 (Oct. 6, 1966), 34.

"Politics for Every Man." *New Republic* 160 (March 8, 1969), 11.

Polsby, Nelson. "Decision Making at the National Convention." *Western Political Quarterly* 13 (1960), 609.

Pomper, Gerald. "The Concept of Elections in Political Theory." *Review of Politics* 29 (1967), 478.

——. "The Southern 'Free Elector' Plan." *Southwestern Social Science Quarterly* 45 (June 1964), 16.

"The Presidential Nomination: Equal Protection at the Grass Roots." *Southern California Law Review* 42 (Fall 1968), 169.

Rabinove, Samuel. "The Electoral College Enigma." *Midstream*, June–July 1969, p. 50.

Roche, John P. "The Electoral College: A Note on American Political Mythology." *Dissent* 8 (1961), 197.

——. "The Founding Fathers: A Reform Caucus in Action." *American Political Science Review* 55 (1961), 799.

Rosenthal, Albert. "The Constitution, Congress and Presidential Elections." *Michigan Law Review* 67 (1968–1969), 1.

——. "Rooting for the Electoral College." *New Leader* 51 (Oct. 21, 1968), 14.

——. "Some Doubts Concerning the Proposal to Elect the President by Direct Popular Vote." *Villanova Law Review* 14 (Fall 1968), 87.

Scammon, Richard M. "The Electoral Process." *Law and Contemporary Problems* 27 (1962), 299.

"Senate Faces Early Decision on Electoral Reform." *Congressional Quarterly* 28 (April 17, 1970), 1025.

Sickles, Robert J. "The Power Index and the Electoral College: A Challenge to Banzhaf's Analysis." *Villanova Law Review* 14 (Fall 1968), 97.

Silva, Ruth. "Reform of the Electoral System." *Review of Politics* 14 (1952), 394.

——. "State Law on the Nomination, Election, and Instruction of Presidential Electors." *American Political Science Review* 42 (1948), 523.

Sindler, Allan P. "Presidential Election Methods and Urban-Ethnic Interests." *Law and Contemporary Problems* 27 (1962), 213.

"State Power to Bind Presidential Electors." *Columbia Law Review* 65 (1965), 696.

Susman, Thomas M. "State of Inhabitancy of Presidential and Vice Presidential Candidates and the Electoral College Vote." *Texas Law Review* 47 (1969), 779.

Thomas, Joel T. "The Constitutional Limitations upon State Regulation of Its Ballot—*Williams* v. *Rhodes.*" *Ohio State Law Journal* 30 (1969), 202.

Thornton, J. Edward. "An Analysis of Electoral College Reform." *Alabama Lawyer* 39 (1968), 398.

Tobin, Richard L. "Direct Vote and the Electoral College." *Saturday Review* 50 (Feb. 18, 1967), 24.

Tyler, Gus. "Save the Electoral College." *New Republic* 143 (Nov. 28, 1960), 15.

Weaver, Warren, Jr. "The Electoral College: After a Very Slow Burn, Its Days May Be Numbered." *New York Times,* Sept. 21, 1960, p. 6.

Welty, Richard C. "Who Really Elects Our Presidents?" *Midwest Quarterly* 2 (1960), 21.

Wicker, Tom. "In the Nation: One Way to Bring Us Together." *New York Times,* Sept. 14, 1969, p. 13.

——. "In the Nation: Trouble for Electoral Reform." *New York Times,* April 19, 1970, p. 17.

Wilkinson, Donald M., Jr. "The Electoral Process and the Power of the States." *American Bar Association Journal* 47 (1961), 251.

Wroth, L. Kinvin. "Election Contests and the Electoral Vote." *Dickinson Law Review* 65 (1961), 321.

Zeidenstein, Harvey. "The South Will Not Rise Again through Direct Election of the President, Polsby and Wildavsky Not Withstanding." *Journal of Politics* 31 (1969), 808.

Index